AN INFINITE CREATION

Juicy Deception
The Conclusion

By

Ivy Lee

This book is a work of fiction. Names, characters, places, and incidents are the product of the author's imagination or are used fictitiously. Any resemblance to actual events, locales, or persons, living or dead, is coincidental.

Story by Ivy Lee

Cover by Kay Palmentera

Edited by Monique, Ebonie & Cortney

Self-Published through Create Space by Ivy Lee

Printed in the United States of America

ISBN-13:
978-1516887064

ISBN-10:
1516887069

A letter to my supporters,

I call you supporters and not fans because fans go with whoever is relevant at the moment while supporters ride with you until the very end.

My supporters are who I am making this part two for because they had my back and waited patiently for me so I am hoping that you continue to have my back and enjoy the conclusion to Juicy Deception.

I need you all to know that I appreciate you all, the countless emails, the many shout outs on every social network, the ones that took my book and hustled and just continuously keep pushing me to write.

The ones that gave me my first interviews and promoted me, the ones that allowed me to whine and vent about my writers block...the ones that tell me my writing is amazing and to stay focused. Thank you. Without you Ivy Lee wouldn't have went further than close friends and family.

I am forever grateful and humbled and I want you to all know from the bottom of my heart and anyone that really knows me knows what I am saying I mean, I love you all.

Thank you. I hope it was worth the wait.....

REST IN PEACE TO ALL THE ONES WE LOST THIS YEAR..........

PRAY FOR CLEVELAND <216>

Dedication

My Maceo,

Where do I begin when it comes to you? You are my muse, my afflatus, one of my very best friends....

You are one person that no matter what happens I will always love you and nothing and no one could ever change that. When two souls are meant to connect they will and nothing can come between that, no matter where they are...you are so far away, but yet we are so close.

Without you I couldn't have made it where I am when it comes to this writing. You have brought out a major piece of me that was hidden and that so many people love about me. You bring out the best in me and this is dedicated to you.....7/16

With Love always & forever no matter what...

"What possible good can come from ignorance about other people? Learn to tell the lions from the lambs or pay the price………"

-Robert Greene; The 48 Laws Of Power

Black

I tossed the rest of my clothes in my gym bag and zipped it up. I was tired and ready to get home and hit the shower and eat. The gym was quiet today, just a few of the regulars and myself. It allowed me to think and release some stress. My seed would be here soon and I knew Aariona was ready to have him. I was excited to see what an actual product of me would finally look like. I was hoping when I got to the house that she had cooked because I was hungry as hell.

Aariona had been tired a lot lately as she got closer to her due date and has been sleeping more and more. I didn't mind because I loved taking care of her and I couldn't wait for her to meet my mother. I just hoped she was able to take that drive with me to go pick her up from jail next week.

"Alright, Dev, man. See you tomorrow." Calvin said.

I gave him a slight head nod and headed to my car. Calvin was this dude I met when I first found a nice home in Pembroke Pines, Miami. He was this over friendly ass neighbor. At first the nigga was irritatin' the hell out of me because after the shit I went through I ain't trust nobody, but this dude wasn't like the niggas I was used to being around so I gave the nigga a chance. He showed us around and he and his wife and Aariona and I would kick it together from time to time. He introduced me to the gym and I found it to be a good way to relieve stress, so I been there three times a week for the past six months and so far so good. At times I wonder what everybody in Cleveland been doing and how much money I been missing.

I pulled up in my driveway and opened the garage and pulled in. Aariona car was still here so I figured she didn't go get the baby some clothes like she planned to. I hope she at least cook because she know I can't boil water. The house was dark and I didn't smell any food and I knew then it was take out night. "Baby!" I called out walking through the kitchen to the living room. I went to cut on the light and called her name one more time. "Aariona!"

I heard someone clapping their hands slowly. *Clap. Clap. Clap.* I walked down the hall and glanced in our bedroom; it was dark too. I stopped for a moment and my heart pounded a little faster because something felt different. I looked in my son's room and there was a man sitting in the rocking chair that I didn't notice at first glance. I looked a little harder.

"Bishop?" I asked.

"What's up little brother?" he asked with a slight laugh.

He didn't even look the same. His eye looked lazy and his nose looked a little lopsided. I instantly got irritated and on a defense. This shit felt fishy.

"Man, where the fuck is my wife and what the fuck you clappin' fo'?"

"Whoa, whoa, whoa, chill little brother." Bishop said throwing his hands in the air as if to say he surrender.

"What wife? You married now? Nah you can't be." He said with slight sarcasm in his voice and a sneaky smirk on his face.

"You can't be 'cause your big brother wasn't even invited to the fuckin' weddin'!" he shouted.

"Fuck the bull shyt nigga, where the fuck is she?" I said immediately pulling out my gun.

I knew Bishop and I knew him well. I know the mind games he plays right before he kills someone; we used to kill together. My heart started racing thinking about how he already probably hurt my wife. I felt anger rise up inside me and I moved closer to his face with my gun.

"Where the fuck is she?" I asked again. This time letting him know that I wasn't playing with him.

He raised his hands higher showing me he wasn't trying to let the situation escalate.

"Chill little brother, I'm only here for my money."

I became confused. "Money? What money?" I asked as I lowered my gun.

Bishop shook his head slowly with an evil ass grin on his face.

"Nigga, the fuckin' money you stole from us!" he shouted. "We was a team! Nigga we was fuckin' family and you pull this shyt?"

I still had no idea what he was talking about. I had been out of contact with everyone from Cleveland for months so I couldn't pinpoint what he even meant.

"Nigga I don't know what the fuck you talkin' 'bout!" I snapped back.

"Dev man, I know you mad at me about Juicy ass and I'm sorry, but I'm not even with her no more. I ended that shyt for you man." He said.

The shyt didn't even sound believable. His faggot ass probably ended it to be with his bitch ass boyfriend. He still didn't know I knew about that. I cringed at the thought of it again.

"Fuck all that nigga. I don't give a fuck about that

bitch," I said. "Where the fuck is my wife? I asked switching the subject to the real issue at hand.

I tried to make sure I showed no emotion or weakness. I knew what Bishop was looking for. He was studying me to find a way inside, anyway he could find. I knew because that's what he taught me to do to nigga when we were in the streets together.

He used to tell me to never break eye contact. Never show any emotion not even anger. Watch their every move, hand gestures, which direction they looked in at any given time; whether it was up, down, right, or left. As soon as they break contact with you in anyway, you got them; you are in full control of them and the situation and can get them to do what you want them to do.

I kept my hand as steady as possible and tried to stay as calm as I could. He already knew I cared for her because I referred to her as my wife repeatedly. I knew that was my first mistake; but I couldn't let him see how deep down my insides felt as though they were tearing into shreds because of the thoughts of her being dead especially while she is pregnant with my son. This feeling was killing me.

I could tell he was trying to see how far he could take this so I decided to speed up the process. I cocked my gun to let him know the seriousness in the situation.

Bishop's eyes enlarged. I knew I had him then. He showed the first sign of emotion before I did which made him the weaker one right now. He showed my favorite emotion; fear. Immediately I could see he regretted it.

I loved when a nigga showed that he feared me. It always gave me the sense of power and power made my dick hard.

"Dev man, all I want is my money. I didn't come here for this shyt." He said.

The cockiness he had when I first got home wasn't in his voice anymore. He seemed unsure of himself; or maybe it was me he was unsure of. Either way, I own him right now and I loved it.

The adrenaline began to rush through my body. I felt this familiar feeling I once loved. I felt like the old me again; the Black that people feared and respected in Cleveland. Here I was just Devon. No one here even knew who "Black" was or what I was really capable of. I felt myself ready to kill him and it felt good.

All I wanted to do was pull the trigger. I just wanted and needed to hear the sound of the bullet leave the barrel and pierce his flesh. I needed to watch him fall to his knees and beg *ME* for his life as if I was God. Right now I was *his* God. I needed this as bad as a crack head needed his pipe.

I could feel my shoulders going at ease as I slipped back into what I know; an old habit that has being trying to die, but hasn't.

The more I watched Bishop lose himself in wondering what I was going to do next, the cockier I became.

This was a nigga that taught me everything I know. A nigga I once loved and looked up to; but in front of me right now, all I see is a bitch ass scary faggot that I have no problem with putting a bullet in his head.

"Nigga you brought this shyt on yourself. You forgot who the fuck I am or somethin'?" I asked him.

"You thought you was gon' come punk me like I'm one of them bitch ass niggas back in Cleveland?"

"Nigga I'm ME! That shyt don't fuckin' change no matter what city I'm in!" I yelled as I moved in closer to him.

"Now where – the – fuck – is –she?" I asked this time refraining from calling her my wife and letting him know that the game was over and it was now my show.

"Did you steal the money Dev?" he asked calmly.

"Nigga *WHAT* fuckin' money? I yelled out of irritation.

"Nigga, you out here livin' it up *right* after we get robbed, disappear; not one mutha fuckin' nigga seen you or heard from you." He said keeping his hands in the air.

He stopped with the games he came attempting to play and finally said what he came to say because he could sense his time coming to an end.

As bad as I didn't want to disturb the area we lived in because this was not the place for it, but when it comes to Aariona I have no limits and I don't give a fuck where I'm at.

"Nigga, all that you see *here, I* paid for with my *money*." I said as calm as I could.

"What the fuck I gotta steal from you for?" I asked.

Bishop looked around. "You tellin' me you was getting' *this* much money Dev?" he asked.

"Nigga, you was fuckin' there! Don't fuckin' count my pockets!" I said getting irritated.

"Some niggas make money and spend it impressin' these bum ass bitches." I said widening my eyes to let him know I was in reference to him. "I stacked my money to get away from them same bum ass bitches."

I felt myself explaining too much to him so I immediately shut my mouth to keep control of the situation.

Bishop stared me in my eyes. I knew then that he was trying to see if I was lying or not. Part of me wanted to just shoot his ass right then and there, but I knew I would never find Aariona if I did that; so I allowed the nigga to read me for a minute in hopes that he saw I wasn't lyin' and give her back to me.

"I believe you little brother." He said.

I stopped myself from saying I don't give a fuck if you do or don't, but I quickly remembered he still had the upper hand over me. He must be getting rusty because he had the real control this entire time, but all he stayed focusing on was the fact that I had a gun in his face.

"Where is she?" I asked for the last time.

Bishop left his hands in the air and grabbed a cell phone with his right hand off the dresser. He moved as slow as he could trying not to set me off as he kept eye contact. He handed the phone to me slowly.

I was confused. "That's not mine."

"It is now. Since it wasn't you that took the money, we need to find out who it was." He said.

"*We*?" I asked as I raised an eyebrow. "What the fuck that got to do with me? "

"Because you the nigga they framed obviously, so I think it would be in yo' best interest to find out who the fuck it really was." He said.

I immediately became defensive. "*My* best interest?"

"Dev you know this shyt bigger than you and me. You aint new to this shyt. It's too much money involved." He said trying to convince me.

I have to admit if I was being blamed for the shyt who the fuck was it that really got them for the money. True enough some of the money belonged to me, but it wasn't hurtin' my pockets. It obviously was hurting Bishops' in a major way though. He spent months searching for me and came a long way to find me.

As he kept his hands up he moved slowly toward the door to leave but kept eye contact.

As he got closer to the hallway leading out of my son's room he said, "She's in the closet.

My heart dropped. I had been in that room this whole time and never heard a sound. I was standing right next to the closet.

"I'm sorry Dev." He said as he continued to back out of the room and move down the hallway.

"Answer when I call." He said and backed out of the house as I followed him with my gun still pointed in his direction.

I watched him get inside of the passenger seat of an all-black BMW with tented windows. He didn't come to Miami alone. I wondered who was in the driver seat.

I looked around to see if any of the neighbors were out because that car would definitely draw attention in this neighborhood.

Once it pulled off I slammed the door and ran back into my son's bedroom. I stopped in front of his closet and paused for a minute feeling my heart beat 100 miles per hour. I couldn't move. I just stared at the closet door thinking the worse. How could she be in there when I didn't hear a sound?

I slowly opened the door and turned on the closet light. There was my beautiful wife balled up with her feet duct taped together. Her hands were also duct taped together behind her back. Her mouth was duct taped with the tape wrapped around her entire head. It looked as if he wrapped it two or three times.

She had tears streaming down her face and snot all over her. She had to have been in there awhile because she was sweating and her eyes were blood shot red.

I kneeled down in front of her. This was the weakest I ever felt. I felt defeated and powerless. I promised her that I would I always protect her and I didn't. I failed her. She looked at me and more tears followed the last. My heart started to sink in my chest.

I felt anger rising up inside of me. I started to remove the tape from her hands slowly. She would jerk her body as I pulled it off and I knew she was in pain. I felt tears slowly go down my cheeks as I continued to remove the tape.

When I finally got to her mouth and removed the tape she let out a loud wail as if she was in so much pain.

Pain that I knew wasn't so much as physical, but emotional and mental pain. A pain that I could never take away from her and that made me feel less of a man.

She grabbed hold of me clenching around my neck screaming and crying as I picked her up. I felt her entire bottom was soaked. Not only did he hurt her, but he took away her dignity. She had peed all over herself.

I wasn't for sure who took the money, but I was for sure of one thing; I was going back to Cleveland for one thing and one thing only; to kill Bishop.

Tiffany

I looked over next to my bed at my daughter as she slept. I was still swollen from giving birth to her almost two months ago. She was born 7lbs 8oz 20 inches long with a head full of curly black hair. She had these slanted eyes that were a light brown and wide. She was a shade darker than me; I'm assuming she is a mixture between myself and Black.

She was beautiful, but no matter how hard I tried, I just didn't feel connected to her at all. People always said that it would come once she was born, but it still hasn't developed even after two months of seeing her every day. I think that she could feel that I didn't feel connected to her at times by the way she would look at me.

I wanted to though. I've tried plenty of times. I just don't think it's in me. I can't see how so many girls want a baby. She has done nothing for me since she has been born except distort my body, made me lose countless nights of sleep and wake me early in the morning every day. I was surprised she was sleeping now.

I was hoping my mother would hurry home from work before she awoke so that I didn't have to pretend with her today. I would rather her to be loved by my mother than to not feel any from me at all.

I still couldn't find Black. He has no idea that he has a daughter now. I wondered if he would even love her if he knew.

She looks so much like him its crazy. I know how much he wanted a kid after finding DJ wasn't his. I heard it devastated him. I thought it was funny the more I thought about how Juicy tried so hard to come between us and he was never his son anyway. I hadn't seen her too often after we robbed their stash house.

As I lay there looking at the ceiling reflecting on that day I still couldn't believe we got away with that shyt. It was such a rush. They never knew what hit them and us getting away with a little over 60k a piece between the three of us? I know they still shook behind that shyt.

I know they're still lookin' for it tho'. It was no way they gon' let 180k just go like that. Word around Cleveland was that Black set the shyt up since he disappeared right when it happened.

The shyt sounded like a good idea at the time; setting him up and framing him, but that was before I known about Teonna. Even though she didn't have a loving mother she didn't deserve to have her father set up and possibly murdered for what I did.

The more I thought about it the more I realized I wasn't shyt. Something had to shake. I had to get myself together. I got up and put my corset on. I was determined to get my small waist back, but I didn't mind the extra weight on my hips Tionna gave me.

I stared in the mirror for a while and the reflection looking back at me was a person I didn't like very much. I wasn't the same person I once loved. The person looking back at me looked so different to me. She wasn't as sweet as she used to be; there was no more innocence about her.

The reflection I saw was now a grown woman. Not just any grown woman; a grown woman that didn't look back and think of her mistakes and what she had done as being wrong, but more as a means to survival.

A woman who honestly deep in her heart believes she was left with no other choice but to do what she did. A woman that if she could do it again and get away with it, she would without so much as blinking an eye.

I had no soul anymore. I definitely sold it for this life and I didn't even care. The softness from my face no longer existed. I could see the cold hearted, loveless emotion in my own eyes so I know it was present when others looked at me.

I had not one single care in the world any longer

and I didn't trust or give a fuck about any nigga breathing. They were all the same to me and at first chance I would set up the next walkin' bank I could.

Sixty thousand was a lot of money for a 19 year old, but it wasn't enough for *this* 19 year old. I wanted more and I was going to get it. I never believed it was *that* much cash flowin' thru Cleveland until I went and got it.

Black was gone; Bishop and Juvey wasn't pushin' the weight they used to and niggas had been layin' low since that jack move we pulled so I really wasn't sure who was out here getting' it for real.

All the lame niggas would post shyt on Instagram like they makin' moves, but I knew better. I knew firsthand the niggas who *really* gettin' it ain't postin' shyt on any network. Shyt some of them don't even have a social network so the only way for me to find where the real money was at was to hit the streets.

Teonna began to squirm in her bassinet breaking my concentration. I sucked my teeth and rolled my eyes. Just then I heard my mother come in the house. *Right on time* I thought to myself.

I threw on my gray *Pink* by Victoria Secret jogging suit and all white Air-Max putting my hair in a neat pony tail.

Even though I didn't know who was gettin' the money in Cleveland right now, I knew one person who did know; my Uncle.

"Hey Tiff!" my mom said walking in my room right past me and to my daughter smiling.

Teonna must have heard her voice because she woke up and smiled at her. I gave a half smile at the way she looked at my mom, then caught myself right away.

"Hey Grandma's baby!" she said smiling as she picked her up.

I realized at that moment why I couldn't connect to Teonna. She makes me feel again and that is one thing I refuse to do. If I began to feel anything it will distract me from doing what I *need* to do.

I snapped back into the *new* Tiffany quickly. The old Tiffany was dead.

"I'm out." I said as I rushed out of the room before she could say anything.

At times I know it gets on her nerves that I just leave like I do, but I know she would rather Teonna stay with her than be with me in these streets.

I have to go see my uncle so I hopped in my Altima and sat there for a minute. I started to question myself.

Fuck! Why did I even look at that kid face? I tried

my hardest to snap back, but for the some reason today it wasn't as easy as it usually is.

I turned my music on as *Recognize* by *PartyNextDoor* featuring *Drake* blasted through the speakers. Fuck it. I love the little girl. I'll admit. I'm doing this for her I attempted to convince myself and ignore the real reason I was doing what I'm doing.

It had absolutely nothing to do with Teonna. It was because I'm greedy and selfish as fuck, but saying it was for her made it sound so much better.

I reversed out of the driveway and headed to Richmond Heights to see my uncle. He didn't know I was coming, but I was sure he would be down to get some money with me.

I was going to call first, but it had been a few months since we spoke and he wasn't too happy with me then so I needed to see him face to face to convince him of the *new* me.

I hit the freeway to take 90 east from 55th. The 30 minute drive should give me enough time to come up with something to say, but hell where do I begin?

Juicy

"Damn, jus' like that." Tae moaned as he grabbed the sides of my hair with both hands and began to gyrate his hips as I was massaging his member with my tonsils. He leaned his head back as I continued to suck and slurp all over him.

Tae loved how I gave him head. I had no gag reflex and I always made it sloppy; just the way he liked it. I was on my knees in doggy style position as he watched my ass I began to bounce it for him while looking him in his eyes the entire time. I felt him get harder inside my mouth. I loved how he watched me. He always made me feel sexy.

Tae, Deontae is his real name, is this dude I met a few months ago when I was at The Vada night club; which is one of the hottest spots to kick it in Cleveland, with one of my girls from the Valley I grew up with.

At first I was reluctant to talk to him, but he was persistent and wasn't taking no for an answer. I had watched him the whole night and he never approached any other female *but* me. They were checkin' for him, but he wasn't paying them any attention.

Tae stood about 6'4", caramel color with deep dimples. He had the prettiest straight white teeth I had ever seen and that's what I liked about him the most. He had on some dark True Religion jeans with some Gucci shoes, Gucci belt and a cream True Religion shirt. He wore his hair in a fade with brush waves. When he walked over to me his cologne had my panties wet almost immediately right after he flashed that smile. I tried to seem uninterested, but our chemistry was too much for me.

I had on a black skin tight dress by Michael Kors that stopped right below my ass, showing my curves and my Christian Louboutin red bottom heels made my ass sit up so much higher in the dress. I wore my hair down with loose body curls. My hair had grown a lot since it was cut from where the stiches were. It was hard for him and me to resist each other, but I kept my cool.

We exchanged numbers and have been together ever since. I enjoyed him. He was different than what I was used to and he was older than me by 10 years. I loved that. I needed a more mature man in my life right now.

He didn't have any kids, which was a major bonus and he worked so much that I never seen him around any other female, but his kin. There wasn't any drama with Tae at all. Everything was always black and white with him. He always said what he mean and means what he says. It was such a turn on to me. I never have to guess what he is thinking because he will tell me on his own.

Whatever Tae asked me for I did it without a question or second guess. I was falling in love with him so fast and it was scary for me.

"Ahhhhh, got damn Juicy!" he screamed as his grip on my hair got tighter.

I felt him explode inside my mouth as the warmth of him shot down my throat. I just continued to suck and swallow until he pushed me off of him to where he couldn't take it any longer.

"Ah, ah, ah, stop girl!" he said laughing and out of breath keeping me at arm's reach with both of his hands on my shoulders.

I seductively licked my lips and bit my bottom lip as I sat up and leaned back on my legs while they were still folded. I postured my body up straight to make sure my stomach stayed looking flat with my arch in my back.

I wasn't shy about my body at all. I *knew* I was sexy and a major turn on for men so I didn't rush to cover up. I wanted him to keep looking at me. I loved the attention.

Tae stared me in my eyes with a smirk on his face. "You swallowed it all, huh?"

I nodded.

He laughed as he shook his head. "What am I gonna do wit' you Juicy?"

I shrugged.

"Damn, girl. You think we movin' too fast?" he asked.

I stopped smiling. "You cum in my mouth, watch me swallow all of your babies and *now* you think we movin' too fast Deontae?"

"Chill." He said as he stopped smiling too. "I jus' asked a fuckin' question. Don't fuck up the mood." He said as he reached over on my night stand and grabbed a blunt that I rolled for him earlier.

I eased up because I could tell he was getting irritated. I didn't want him to leave and the last time we almost argued he left. He didn't respond to me he just walked out and didn't talk to me for two days.

"What time is your son comin' home?" he asked changing the subject.

"In about an hour." I said quietly.

I knew that meant he was leaving before then. Tae had never met DJ and whenever the school bus dropped him off he always left out the back door of my house so that he couldn't see him when he came in. I wanted them to meet, but Tae said he wasn't ready for that just yet.

After DJ was shot and I was robbed we moved out of The Valley, which something I never planned on doing, and into a small bungalow in Maple Heights. It was okay living here, but The Valley was home to me and I missed it, but because I didn't know who robbed me or had any leads on it, I knew it was time to go.

I stopped boosting like I used to, I didn't stop completely because I'm good at it and it came so natural plus I had some loyal customers that spent money with me for years. Tae didn't know that I boosted and I never planned on telling him. He was a business owner and for some reason I was ashamed to tell him that about me.

He never really asked me questions about my past, which I was glad about because I didn't want to lie to him about anything. My cell began to vibrate on my dresser so I slid off the bed and walked toward it with a switch in my hips because I knew Tae was watching me. I kept my back to him so that he could stare at my ass.

When I picked up my phone I had two missed calls from Bishop and a text. I frowned my face. At one point in time I would have smiled at the sight of his name calling me when I was crazy about him and now I regret the fact that he is the biological father of DJ.

I opened the text only to get much more irritated. All he and I do now is argue and fight. If we aren't arguing about DJ and how he wants me to change his name I'm listening to him yell about how *somebody* robbed him and who told on his mama to the FEDs.

Stalyce has been on lock for months now. It was her own fault from what I heard, but let Bishop tell it she was snitched on. In Cleveland niggas never accepted responsibility for the shyt they did, it was always someone else's fault. At times I missed Stalyce and our friendship and some days I wanted to reach out to her, but my pride stopped me every time.

I even missed Peaches; Black's mom because over the years with me going to see her and writing her all the time we developed a bond, but I couldn't face her after the truth came out. I never even bothered to ask Black if he told her the truth.

I knew that he liked to keep negative shyt away from her so all she ever heard was the good when it came from his way. He was so protective over her.

I started to call Bishop back, but I have never talked to him in front of Tae before or any other man for that fact and I wasn't sure how he would react. He didn't have any children of his own so I didn't think he would understand even if I explained it was strictly about DJ.

He knew who Bishop was and he knew what his

reputation from the streets was so I just steered clear of it and put the phone back on my dresser and went back to the bed with Tae. I didn't have much time left with him so I had to enjoy it.

"Something wrong?" he asked.

I pierced my lips together as I shook my head and climbed on top of him and sat down. "Nah, I'm good."

He stared me in my eyes, but didn't say a word. He inhaled some more of the blunt I rolled him and put it to my lips as he exhaled, but never breaking the stare. I felt like he was trying to read me, something that Black used to do all the time and I hated it.

"I wanted to say something, but instead I took a deep inhale of the weed then leaned toward his face as I exhaled it into his mouth then began to kiss him as deep as I could. I felt myself getting wetter as I slowly began to grind my clit onto him. I could feel him becoming erect again which turned me on even more.

He set the weed down on the night stand and took both of his hands as he ran them up through my hair, pulling me closer to him.

Our breathing began to pick up as our kissing became intense. I could feel him in my soul as he kissed me and held me tightly. I leaned up slightly; never breaking our kiss, as I took my left hand and slid him inside me slowly.

I was soaked by then and as soon as he entered me we both let out moans simultaneously as he gripped my hair with both of his hands. The grip that he had turned me on even more.

"Damn, Juicy…..this pussy so good baby." He moaned.

I smirked and bit on his bottom lip seductively as I picked up the pace riding him.

"Slow down." He moaned.

I slowed down to allow him to collect himself and as soon as he was relaxed I gripped him while he was deep inside me. I felt my walls tighten around his member and he closed his eyes and moaned louder this time.

I watched him try and keep himself from bussing, but this was my show. I owned this dick right now and I wanted to make sure I stayed on his mind after he left.

I hear women say pussy can't keep a man, but them must be the hoes that don't know how to work theirs because mine sure as hell keeps them coming.

I continued to squeeze my muscles as tight as I could; just like when I'm using my Ben-Wa balls and I felt myself cumming from the penetration. I started to ride him faster because I knew once he felt how warm it was getting between that and my pace he was going to cum right after me.

See the reason women aren't satisfied in bed is because they don't take the time to get to know their own body. I know my body and how to make myself cum because if you don't get yours before he gets his you just shyt out of luck and I am never willing to take that chance.

"AAAAHHHHH SSSHHHYYTTT!" he yelled as he came as soon as he felt me cum which made me cum a second time.

I screamed as we both climaxed and grabbed each other tightly as I collapsed on top of his chest. We couldn't move nor say a word. We just lay there attempting to get our breathing under control.

I paused on my breathing as I listened to his heart beat through his chest. I hugged him tighter as I closed my eyes to enjoy the moment. I was in love.

There was no fighting it, I knew I wanted him and I would do whatever I had to do to keep him. I knew the only way to keep him was to play by his rules; for now.

As I hugged him tighter his arms closed in on me holding me as tight as I was holding him. I felt so secure and I loved this feeling. I kept my eyes closed as I dozed off right in his arms.

I wasn't sure how long we had been sleep, but the sound of a loud horn in front of my house awoke us both. It was DJ's school bus. I jumped up and threw on my tank and shorts that were lying next to the bed on the floor.

My room reeked of kush and sex. The horn began to seem louder as I rushed to find my flip flops. Tae began to dress as I was under the bed reaching for my other shoe.

He didn't bother to help me find my shoe nor did he go to the door to signal to let the driver know that I was on my way out. I rolled my eyes at him as I finally found my shoe and walked out the room. He didn't seem to care at all he continued to take his time dressing.

I knew the driver was only impatient because he was holding up traffic to let DJ off the bus and it sometimes took a few extra minutes to get his wheel chair off the bus.

My baby never was back 100% after he was shot. He had to learn to do so much all over again. When he first came out of the coma he seemed fine, as if everything would be getting better, but then one day he reverted back and couldn't stand up straight, couldn't walk, couldn't hold a cup or even write.

I blamed the doctors for lying to me. They never said that this could happen. They gave me false hope that when he came out of the coma he would be good as new. It was the total opposite. Now he has been in therapy for the last two months.

Bishop blames me for it. I guess he forgot that it was *his* mother that put DJ in harm's way as *he* was fuckin' my brains out in *his* apartment. DJ doesn't even remember being shot. He doesn't remember being in the hospital and he has never mentioned Black to me so I assumed he didn't remember him either, which made it easier to tell him that Bishop was his father.

"I'm sorry, I fell asleep." I said to the bus driver as I helped him take DJ off the bus.

"This is becoming routine with you." The elderly man said lecturing me.

I knew he was upset with me because I have had many excuses as to why I'm always late to get DJ off the bus. I ignored him and directed my attention straight to DJ.

"Hey mommy's lil' man." I said smiling as I rolled his chair toward the house.

"This is the last day for this!" the bus driver yelled to my back.

"Okay!" I yelled back at him never turning back around.

I heard him mumble something as he got onto the bus and pulled off. I didn't care. My high was coming down and I was starving. I thought about how this was my chance to get Tae and DJ to finally meet as I walked him up the ramp to my front door.

Bishop had a ramp built in front of my house once DJ was ordered to a wheel chair. Even though I hated his guts now I couldn't deny he did step up immediately when he found out he is his father. Black was a better father, but Bishop wasn't too bad.

As I entered the house I left DJ in the living room. "I'll be right back baby, it's someone I want you to meet."

I ran into my bedroom smiling only to find Tae not there. I walked back out into the bathroom looking around and then made my way into the kitchen. He wasn't there. I frowned as I walked back to the living room.

Right through the picture window I saw Tae backing out of the driveway and onto the street. I became furious instantly. This was some bull shyt and low of him to do that. He must have slipped out the back door as I was coming through the front door.

Normally I would pick up the phone and call him to cuss him out, but he doesn't carry a cell phone. He was the only nigga I ever met that didn't own a cell phone.

"Who you want me to meet Mommy?" DJ asked as I continued to stare out the window.

"Nobody baby. You hungry?" I asked him redirecting my attention to him.

He nodded. "Yes."

I grabbed the handles of his wheel chair and pushed him into the kitchen trying to hold back my tears. "Okay, baby what do you want to eat?"

Black

There was complete silence around my home the last week and I hadn't slept since Bishop came to my house. I was sitting in my recliner looking out the window trying to piece it altogether. Some shyt just wasn't adding up to me.

The more I replayed the day and every detail in my head over and over the angrier I would get. It's bull shyt to try and change your life because the past always has a way of finding you.

I could barely look Aariona in her eyes. She didn't say much to me at all either. I knew this situation would change her, but it really changed us. She stayed away from me for a few days.

I followed her to make sure she was ok because I didn't trust Bishop at all and most of the time she would just go to the park and sit or walk around.

She hadn't mentioned our son like she did before. Her energy she had, the energy I needed from her, seemed to have completely disappeared. She seemed lifeless and I hated myself for it.

I told myself over and over that I knew I was no good for her so I should have let her be with someone that wouldn't ever have her in bull shyt like this, but I couldn't live without her. I refused to live without her.

Tomorrow was the day to go pick my mother up from prison and I really wanted Aariona to go with me. We lived half an hour from where she was located in the FEDs at FDC Miami.

Then it dawned on me that's how Bishop found me. I knew the nigga wasn't as good as me when it came to this thinkin' shyt and how to find niggas because I was always the brains behind our business.

I was a natural at it. I learned it from watching my mother as a kid and when she left I took a few lessons from Bishop and Stalyce, but I was always smarter than them both.

I sat straight up in my recliner realizing that he was on some bull shyt deeper than I thought and that it was actually an accident that he came across Aariona and I.

He must have been in Miami waiting for my mother to be released so that he could get to her before I could in attempt to make me come out. It just so happened that he found me first.

I stood up and walked back to my bed room closet and searched for my glock. I don't give a fuck who took his money or whatever his reason was to come to Miami, his life was over. I knew there was no coming back from what I needed to do because he went as far as threatening the life of my family.

I haven't heard from my mother in a few days. I figured it was because they had already shut down everything for processing her since she was about to be released.

I sat on the edge of the bed holding my gun in my right hand and stared at the mirrored closet and looked at my reflection. I was trying to figure out how to tell Aariona that it was time to go.

I had already asked her to give up her entire life for me, her house, her career, and her friends and just leave with me; now I had to ask her to drop her new life she started here with me?

She wasn't built for this lifestyle and I couldn't even bring myself to try and mold her for it. I didn't want her to be built for it. I didn't want her to change at all. Her being different is what I needed and loved about her and her innocence she possessed gave me hope. I felt as if she was being tainted the more I stayed in her life.

The cell phone rang that Bishop left for me. I reached inside my basketball shorts and pulled it out.

"Yeah." I said dryly into the phone.

"Little Brother!" Bishop said with too much enthusiasm; as if this was months ago and we were still as close as we once were. I pulled the phone away from my ear and looked at it and shook my head.

"Talk." I said putting the phone back to my ear.

"We need to link up." He said without the extra enthusiasm he called with.

"You still in Miami?" I asked.

"Nah. I'm back in Cleveland." He said.

I took a slight sigh of relief. If he was gone then that meant he wasn't going after my mother as I thought. He still was going to pay for what he did to Aariona, but at least he knew better than to fuck with my mother.

"I'll be there in a few days." I said.

"Nah, that's too long." He said.

"I got shyt goin' on here right now, I need a few days." I said not backing down.

"Two days, Dev." Bishop said as he hung up on me.

I slid the phone back in my pockets and dropped my head. I just want to get away from this shyt. I made the money I wanted to make, my mother was coming home, I had my wife and my son was coming soon; I just want to enjoy it.

Just as I was sitting there feeling myself fill up with anger and rage Aariona walked in slowly and stood in front of me. She didn't say a word. I wondered had she been listening to me on the phone she was so quiet.

I realized I still had my gun in my hand, she had never seen me with it. I always tried to keep it away from her. This was the closet she had come to me since Bishop had tied her up.

I looked up at her into her eyes as I slowly put the gun behind me. She had on a long strapless blue summer dress. Her feet were out and had a French tip on them to match her nails. She had her hair in a messy bun on top of her head with these diamond earrings I bought her.

Her Versace perfume smelled so good to me and I wasn't sure if it was the pregnancy or her tan that made her glow, but she was beautiful.

She took her left hand and put it on my cheek. I closed my eyes. It was something about her touch that made all the bull shyt disappear for a minute.

She leaned in and kissed my lips softly. I opened my eyes as she pulled back and put my hand on top of her hand that she had on my face. I felt her wedding ring and looked at it then back at her.

Aariona hadn't wore her ring in a few weeks. She said her hand was hurting from it swelling so she took it off. She was still swollen, but she put it on anyway. I knew that was her way of showing me that she was still here. That she still loved me and still wanted to be my wife.

"Still?" I asked.

She nodded. "Always."

I stood up and put both of my hands behind her head and pulled her in to kiss me. I kissed her deeper than I have ever kissed her.

"I'm going to protect you," I said reassuring her. "You and my son."

"I know." She said. "I've never doubted you, I was just scared."

"I'm so sorry for that. For all of this." I said hoping she would forgive me completely.

"I know." She said.

"Will you still go with me to get my mother?" I asked praying she would say yes.

"Yes." She said as she rested her head on my chest. I stood there holding her tightly as she held me too. We needed each other. I felt my son giving light kicks as I was holding her.

"Devon?" she asked still resting her head.

"Yeah?"

"Who was that man that tied me up?" she finally asked me.

"Bishop."

"Your brother?" she asked.

"Yes." I said reluctantly because that is how she knew who he was to me.

"Have I ever asked you for anything?" she asked.

I shook my head. "Nah. Never. But if you did I would give you anything you asked for you know that."

"Anything?" she asked.

"Anything." I reassured her.

"I want him dead." She said as she looked me in my eyes.

I knew there was going to be a change in her, but not to this extent. I was going to kill him anyway, but the fact that she asked me to do it, I *had* to now.

I stared into my wife's eyes. I was trying my hardest to read her. I never imagined seeing her eyes so empty and so cold. She meant what she was asking me to do there was no doubt about it. She had to have been thinking about it too because she waited almost a week to ask me to do this.

"Devon?" she said.

I was hesitant about answering her this time because I never expected the first thing to ever come from her. "Yeah?"

"I have to watch him die." She said.

I knew she was further gone than I thought, probably more than I even had a clue of.

"Aariona, I have no problem givin' you anything you ever ask me for, but don't let this change you. Stay the same you." I pleaded.

She pulled away from me and started to walk out the room.

"Just do what I asked." She said never looking back at me.

I raised an eyebrow to her smart ass mouth because it caught me off guard, but I didn't say anything. I watched her walk down the hallway until she disappeared into the next room. I wondered where we were going from there.

The next morning I woke up early. I was excited to finally see my mother. I haven't seen her since my 18th birthday. I remember our last visit so vividly.

"You are so handsome son." She said smiling at me.

My mother, Peaches, stared me in my face. She was the most beautiful woman I had ever seen. She had the smoothest, creamy cocoa skin. She was wearing her hair slicked to the back in a ponytail. She always had the nicest smile and her right cheek possessed just one dimple. She stood about 5'5" and was in shape. She didn't get her figure from jail. She walked in there with it, but she didn't lose it either.

She had been there a few years already, and she seemed to be maintaining, but this visit was different. I felt it by the way she was staring at me.

"What's wrong Ma?" I asked picking up on the vibe.

"You can't come see me here no mo'." She said.

"Huh?" I asked immediately getting upset.

"Listen to me, aight?" She said looking me in my eyes.

I never questioned my mother when she told me to do something, I just did it, but this time I had to question her.

"Why? Yo' you can't jus' say that and not say why, Ma." I said almost begging her.

"Get yourself together." She said snapping at me and leaning closer to me. "You can't allow your emotions to show like you doin' right now. This is a dog eat dog world and that shyt you showin' right now shows weakness and they will eat you alive." She said staring me in my eyes.

We never broke eye contact and I quickly collected myself. She nodded as she noticed me doing what she instructed me to do.

"Devon, don't trust anyone around you at all." She said. "You understand me?"

I nodded.

"Now I need you to stop the visits, but I will still call. Stay out the way from the bull shyt, save your money and get

the fuck out." she said.

I nodded again. I didn't interrupt her at all.

"Do exactly what I tell you and you will be fine. Don't spend your money on these bitches and leave the weed alone. A sober mind thinks better; makes wiser choices and you can see your enemies a mile away."

I nodded again.

"Don't let anyone know your next move; not even me. When you learn new information about your circle, it stops with you, never repeat it whether it's good or bad; understand? You don't ever need confirmation. Trust your gut, that's your confirmation." she said still staring me in my eyes.

"Yes, ma'am." I replied.

"I will see you when I touch down. And no matter what happens, look out for DJ." She said.

"Of course, Ma, that's my son." I said.

She didn't say a word. She just stared at me. "I love you son." She said as she stood up and ended our visit.

Deep down inside I wanted to cry. I wanted to scream and throw every table and chair around that visiting room, but that would have went against everything she just told me not to do. That was the last time I saw my mother.

I looked over at the alarm clock after I reminisced about our last encounter and saw it was 8:30am. I hopped up and jumped in the shower. As happy as I felt I was also nervous.

I didn't know what to wear as if this was my first time I was meeting her. I started to get my emotions in check, but then I thought about it, this is the first time I get to hug my mother without anyone telling us to stop in years and the first time Aariona gets to meet her mother in law. She would just have to understand that emotions would be seen today.

"Aariona!" I yelled from the bathroom. "You dressed?"

"Yeah, meet you in the car." She yelled back.

"Ok, we have to hurry up, she doesn't know we comin'. I want to get to her before she gets on the bus."

"Okay!" she said.

I quickly dressed and ran to the car.

"Excited?" she asked.

"I'm good." I said lying.

Aariona didn't say another word she just reclined her seat and laid back.

We pulled up to the prison just as other inmates were leaving. I saw majority walking to the bus, while only two others were getting picked up. I scanned the crowd looking for my mother, but didn't see her.

"You sure she getting out today?" I asked Aariona

whom was the one that checked for me. She nodded.

"Can you go find out while I wait a little longer out here and see if she comes out?" I asked her.

She nodded and struggled to get out of the passenger seat. I watched her wobble to the door, but continued to look around the crowd to see if I saw her.

About 20 minutes later Aariona came back out and I watched the bus pull off. I was sitting on the hood of my car wondering what was taking them so long.

"Well?" I asked. "Wrong date?"

"Apparently. She was released a few days ago." She said.

My eyes widened. "What? They can do that?"

"I guess so. But why wouldn't she have called you of all people by now?"

I started to answer her then quickly shut my mouth as I remembered what my mother told me before about talking too much. I started to think as I used only my eyes to look around the parking lot again, but kept my head still facing Aariona.

Either Bishop had my mother or she was up to something. And if my mother is the same woman that taught me the game, she was definitely up to something. I refuse to believe she would allow a fuck nigga like Bishop do somethin' to her.

"Let's go baby." I said to Aariona as I hopped off the hood of the car.

"What about your mother?" she asked.

"Let's go." I repeated and got in the driver side.

Tiffany

"What the fuck you want, Tiff?" Unk said as he was going inside his back security door never looking directly at me. I followed behind him to try and plead my case to him.

Unk had a laid out spot out in Richmond Heights. Even though he didn't live in the hood no more, he still *acted* like he lived in the hood.

His crib was big as hell. The whole yard was gated and there was a security door to the patio door that lead to another security door. He had cameras everywhere along his property. I really didn't know how he slept at night knowing he had to watch his back, even living out here.

He had done so much dirt just to live the life he was living and when I was younger I would judge him in my mind often wondering how he could do what he did. I would tell myself I would never do the things he did to get money. I never thought I was that grimy. But it must be genetic because the shyt felt so natural to me now.

"Unk, I need to talk." I said grabbing the heavy security door before it closed on me.

He continued to unlock the other door, still never looking me in the eyes. I heard his pit-bulls barking from the inside. I hated his dogs. They were trained to kill and I was always afraid that one day they would attack me even though I've been around them since they were puppies.

"Nothin' you have to say interest me, Tiff." He said as he walked through his kitchen patting his dogs as he went to the fridge.

I locked the door behind me and stood next to the door. The kitchen looked different since the last time I was there. He was always switching up his house. Everything was now stainless steel and his kitchen floors were some kind of marble design. As I glanced around he grabbed himself a bottle of water and leaned against the sink and began to sip it.

I fell in love with his house immediately and I knew then that coming there wasn't a mistake because this is the kind of house I wanted for me. For me and Teonna. This was my own personal corroboration I needed. He looked at me as he took a sip and nodded his eyes toward the bar that he put it across the back door to barricade it.

He never took chances when it came to his safety. He didn't have a reason to barricade his door right now, but he did anyway. I turned around immediately and put the bar up. His dogs walked to his side and one sat on each side of him and both looked my way ready to attack at his first command.

I felt like I was coming before a judge right now. I felt my palms get sweaty and closed the grip on my hands into a loose fist. I tried to seem calm, cool and collected because I knew he was watching my movements.

He raised his eyebrows as if to say, *well*? I couldn't remember what I wanted to say even though I rehearsed it over and over in my mind all the way there.

"First, I guess I wanna say I'm sorry. I fucked up." I attempted to sound sincere.

I wasn't sorry at all. I felt like I earned that money anyway. *I* was the one that dealt with Black and his bull shyt. *I* was the one who came up with the plan. The only thing my Uncle did was point me in the right direction. Which is what I needed him to do again.

"Mmmm." Was all he said.

"Don't do that, I'm tryin' to make this right, Unk." I said.

"You got my money?" he asked cutting straight to the point.

I shook my head.

"So *how* the FUCK can you make it right?" he asked with a harsher tone than he had when I first walked in.

I became afraid. My uncle never cared about the blood is thicker than water rule. I don't think he cared about anyone but himself and my mother. I really felt like the only reason he didn't kill me *was* because of my mother. She was his favorite out of all six of their siblings.

Something happened with his father growing up and she protected him. He and my mother never told the story, but from what I gathered from the rest of their siblings she walked in on their father trying to make my uncle give a nigga some head so he could get high. My mom was older than my uncle and she stabbed the nigga that was about to rape my uncle in the leg with a knife.

He denied it when I asked him, but as angry as he got when it came up I believe it was true. Their dad was some kind of fiend and it was rumored that my Unk is the one that killed him by giving him some bad heroine. He denies that too.

My mother won't even speak on it all she says is "leave my brother alone" when it comes up. She is the only one he is kind too, at least that I ever saw of. I watched him beat the shyt out of his other brother over $100 before so I can only imagine if I wasn't his favorite sisters first born what he would do to me if he found out

I had that money. I actually feared for myself and Teonna if he found out.

"I don't know." I shrugged.

He began to pet his dog's head looking down toward them and taking his attention from me.

"Maybe we can find another nigga to hit up?" I said in a lower voice.

He immediately looked back up at me and stopped rubbing their heads.

"What?" he snapped at me.

"I'm sayin' I didn't know better then, I do now though.

"Where is Black?" he asked ignoring what I said.

I was confused.

"I don't know."

"If you can't complete the first job why the fuck would I have you on another one?" he asked in a calmer tone.

I shrugged.

"Nobody know where he at." I said. "He disappeared.

"It wasn't *nobody* job to know; it was *your* job." He said sarcastically as he folded his arms across his chest.

I had no words. I felt like a child who had just disappointed her parent right now.

"I'm ready." I said.

"Who the kid belong to?" he asked.

I was hesitant to answer.

"Black or the faggot you was fuckin'?" he asked again.

My eyes widened. How did he even know about Juvey? How did he even know he was gay? My uncle was scarier than I ever imagined. He knew so much about me without me ever telling him anything.

"Black's." I said wondering what his point was.

"Then you will never be ready. You will never complete the job because you fucked up the plan and had a baby wit' this nigga." He said looking me in the eyes.

"How you figure?" I asked him knowing he was right about me never turning Black over to him, but anyone else; without hesitation, I would. Hell I didn't even know if we would ever even see Black again so it didn't even matter.

"So you sayin' you don't mind that I rob yo' baby daddy and kill him?" he asked with a devilish side grin.

I didn't like the sound of that scenario. Not because I loved Black, because I was over him completely, but because of Teonna. She deserved to know who her father is.

I didn't answer his question. I just stared back at

him while he read me. I knew my face showed that I wasn't feelin' what he just said and I was ok with that as long as he didn't make me admit it out loud.

"I fucked up." Was my response.

"Let it go, Tiff. This ain't the life for you. Jus' go home take care of your kid and go back to school or somethin'."

I wanted so bad to tell him what I did. What me, Keyona and Juicy did. I wanted to sit him down and tell him how I was the brains behind the whole set up. How I came up with the idea of setting Black up and how we got all that money and nobody suspected us; but I couldn't.

I couldn't share that with him or nobody else. If he knew I did that he would definitely believe that all that money belonged to him and I cut him out the deal somehow.

"I'm ready." I said stepping closer to him.

His dogs both at once stood up on all fours as if they were ready to attack at any given moment when I moved from my space and closer to them. I glanced down at them then back to my uncle.

"Why do you even want Black anyway? That nigga ain't got no money. Didn't you hear how the whole team got robbed?" I asked pretending it was gossip that I heard.

He laughed and shook his head and folded his arms back across his chest.

“The team got robbed. He didn’t.” he said.

“It was his money too.” I said.

He shook his head again. “You really don’t know who you was dealin’ wit’ do you?

“I mean, if he was part of the team and they all got took down then he did too unless he the one that did it.” I tried to convince him I knew what I was talking about. I did my best to play it off like I didn’t know the truth.

“Find me Black and I’ll let you back in.” he said ignoring what I just said to him.

“What about Teonna?” I asked.

“That’s the only way you can come back in; the only way I know you’re serious.” He said without blinking an eye.

I knew this was something I couldn’t do. Not that I wouldn’t do, but I actually couldn’t.

“Do you have to kill him?” I asked just to see if he would at least allow him to have his life still.

He nodded.

“Why? Why can’t you jus’ rob him and let him live?” I asked.

“You ain’t ready.”

"I am, but I have to think about my daughter too, Unk."

"You ain't ready." He repeated.

"I am."

"Will you do it?" he asked.

I nodded. "But how?"

He laughed, "That's your job to find out not mine."

I shook my head. I had no idea where to start. Black wasn't your average street nigga. He was smart. He was a thinker. He could be half way across the country somewhere. I didn't even know his real full name!

"Can't you jus' at least point me in the right direction?" I asked almost begging.

"As many times you fucked this nigga you can't think of one thing he said to you that would give you a clue? Even when he was pillow talkin'?"

I shook my head. "No."

I couldn't think of shyt because he never told me shyt. I learned half what I knew about him at the end of our relationship only because I started following him. He never pillow talked. He never shared too much of anything and I was only 17 how the fuck was I supposed to know it was more that I should have been checkin' for besides the money?

"I don't know what to tell you, Tiff. I told you the stipulations on you comin' back in wit' me."

"Aight." I said not knowing what else to say. He wasn't going to bend this time and it was clear. I had to go back home and figure this shyt out. "I'll call you."

He nodded. "Only when you have somethin' for me. Other than that I don't do social calls."

I stood there and didn't say anything else. He waved his hand as if he was telling me to leave the room.

"Get the fuck out."

I didn't respond I just turned and took the bar off the door and left.

As I walked to my car I kept replaying all the times I spent with Black over and over in my head hoping I could come up with something and I couldn't.

I knew more about Juvey in the short time I was creepin' wit' him than I did in the year I spent with Black.

I knew one woman that did know about Black and even though I didn't want to call her I knew I had to for this. I sat in the driver side of my car and looked around before I dialed her number. We hadn't spoken since the robbery so I wasn't sure what she would say.

I got her voicemail on the first ring.

"Juicy, it's Tiff. We need to talk. Call me soon as you get this."

I hung up the phone and headed back across town hoping, almost praying she would call me back.

Juicy

I lay in my bed naked after my shower feeling lazy. I hadn't spoken to Tae since he left my house the other day. Which wasn't out of the norm with him because of the way he worked.

I was so bored and was thinking about Tae as I scrolled through Instagram looking at all the dumb ass post. Most of them repetitive with different captions, a lot of lames lying about shyt they never seen in person like money and cars, hoes arguing over the same nigga, just dumb silly shyt.

I wasn't a person that posted too often. I was private about my life so it was about ten post on my page at the most. I really didn't know why I had it, probably for moments like these right now.

I had a missed call from Tiffany and even though she and I did what we did together she wasn't a friend or even an associate so I had no idea as to why she was calling me. Her voice mail said to call when I got the message and I been contemplating for the last few days if I even wanted to call her. Since I was bored and Instagram wasn't keeping my interest I decided to return the call.

"Hello?" she answered on the first ring.

"Yo'?" I said.

I couldn't deny after getting to know Tiff she was a cool ass female, but I wasn't interested in being her friend. The bitch was shady to the bone if you asked me. She came up with that plan for us to rob them niggas and it wasn't like it didn't work. We was sitting on their money and not losing any sleep at all because they didn't suspect us. The bitch was smart and grimy. She couldn't be my enemy, but she definitely couldn't be a friend.

"I got some shyt I need to holla at you 'bout." She said.

"Talk." I said wondering what she was on.

"Face to face." she said. "No phones."

I sat up in my bed. Either she had another plan to get some money or they have a feeling it was us.

"Aight, where?" I asked.

"Your house cool?" she asked.

I was hesitant on answering her. She didn't know where I lived, but deep down I knew she wasn't on no bull shyt with me. Maybe her girlfriend was, but not her.

"Jus' you. Don't bring anybody wit' you." I said and she knew I meant Keyona.

"Bet. Text me the address, I'll be there in 15 minutes." She said hanging up.

I text her the address and hopped out of bed. I reached in my drawer and put on a jogging suit and tied my hair up. I don't know why I automatically thought as if something was about to go down, but I wanted to be prepared just in case. I reached underneath my mattress and grabbed my gun. I made sure it was off safety and loaded.

I didn't believe that she would be on no bull shyt, but I wanted to stay prepared because in Cleveland you couldn't trust anyone. I was glad Bishop had DJ for the weekend since she was coming by.

I sat on the edge of the bed and tied my tennis shoes up then walked to the living room and sat on the couch. I put the gun underneath a couch pillow just in case she was being cool I didn't want to scare her off when she saw the gun.

I glanced down at my phone to check the time, 30 minutes later she still wasn't there. The sun was setting and I started to call her back when a white Altima pulled in my driveway. She definitely was spending her money and it was showing. I got up and opened the door for her and she walked in.

For some reason she seemed happy to see me, like when you haven't seen a good friend in a while. I honestly was happy to see her too because after I moved I didn't see much of my friends from the Valley anymore. I wanted to reach in and give her a hug, but I didn't.

"Hey." I said.

"Hey" she said smiling.

She was a really pretty girl. I could see why Black took interest in her even though she was so young. She had put on a few pounds from having her baby, but it looked nice on her.

I closed the front door and pointed toward the sofa. "Have a seat."

She sat down and I followed sitting on the opposite end of the couch.

"So?" I asked skipping small talk.

I think she picked up on my queue and went straight to why she was here.

"Have you heard from Black?" she asked.

I don't know why I felt irritated inside almost immediately. I think partially because of the past she and I had when it came to him and the fact that she knew for sure her kid belonged to him and my son didn't; she still had a piece of him I would never have anymore and I hated it.

"Nah, why?" I asked frowning my face and shaking my head.

"I really need him to know he has a daughter and I can't think of how to get in touch with him." She said.

"So why come to me?" I asked.

"Because you know him better than anybody." She admitted.

I began to feel at ease for some reason. Like I still had one over her when it came to him, even though she was the one with his child.

"I guess." I shot back.

She was quiet as if she was waiting for me to say more to her. We stared each other down for a minute.

"I know you have some idea." She said breaking the silence.

I shook my head.

"Is it that you jus' don't wanna tell me?" she asked.

"I really don't know. His mom is coming home soon I think so maybe he somewhere with her or near her." I said.

"Where is that at?"

"Miami." I said.

She frowned. "He really jus' disappeared. I jus' want him to know about his daughter." She said.

I didn't reply. I just let her talk. She could sense I didn't care about what she was talking about right now or had any interest in helping her and so she stopped talking.

"That's what you wanted to talk 'bout?" I asked rushing her to the point.

"I want to get some more money." She said getting to what I wanted to hear.

I smiled. "Me too. What's the plan?" I asked. I figured she had a new prospect in mind and the way she thinks I was sure we could pull it off. I just hoped she decided to leave her girlfriend behind this time.

"That's what I need *you* to find out." She said.

"I been out the way, I don't know who getting' it right now." I said.

She shook her head and looked down as she rested her elbows on her knees folding her hands together like she was thinking about what I just said to her.

"These bitch ass niggas in Cleveland so fuckin' broke for real. They ain't gettin' it like Black and them was. What 'bout them niggas in EC?" she asked. EC was what we called East Cleveland for short.

I shrugged. "I haven't been that way in a min. I'm sure it's a few over there gettin' it still."

"Who you know over there?" she asked.

"A few niggas." I said not dropping any names. Some of them was already locked up so it was no point in mentioning them.

"But you sure you wanna go over there? Them niggas not like the niggas we robbed. They live for this kinda shyt so it won't be easy as the first time." I said making sure she knew what she was getting into.

"You scared?" she asked.

I shook my head. "Of what?"

"I don't know. You sound scared to me." She said looking me in my eyes almost taunting or daring me.

I sucked my teeth. "Well I'm not."

"All I'm sayin' is they may be ready for this kinda of shyt, but they jus' like any other nigga out here; new pussy always gets to them and we ain't from they way so they gon' easily let us in. We jus' need to know who gettin' it so we can take it. That's all." She said with so much confidence as if it was going to be a walk in the park, but I knew better.

I agreed with what she was saying, but we *knew* the niggas we robbed. We knew where they slept, who they kicked it with, who they family was, friends and all that shyt, we don't know *shyt* about EC niggas except what we heard so I was skeptical.

"How you wanna do that?" I asked entertaining her ideas.

"Let's go to they spots. Hang out, peep the scenery and go from there." She said.

"We can go to the Prive'." I said.

The Prive' was a club right in the middle of EC where they all kicked it at. I heard it jumped especially when they brought out guest like Jeezy and Migos. I just stayed in my lane and never went to their side of town.

"Bet. But not together." She reminded me.

"Same day tho'?" I asked. She nodded.

"Jus' stay in my visual and I'll send you text about

what I see and you do the same, but delete right after you read them. We don't want to take no chances on shyt." She said.

"You right." I agreed, but all the while thinking to myself this lil' hoe the devil. I always thought I was sneaky, but she on another level.

"Aight, well let's do that and go from there." She said standing up. I stood up at the same time with her. I never sat down while anyone was standing over me.

"What day you wanna go?" she asked.

"Let's go on Thursday. They got some night called Wavy Thursdays or some shyt." I said.

"Bet." She said walking toward the door. "Keyona a be with me, but not part of this plan, ok?"

I nodded. "Even better."

She walked out the house and was looking around as she went to her car. I closed the door and leaned against it and laid my head back and looked at the ceiling.

Man what the hell are you doin' Juicy? I said I was done with this shyt and it was a one-time thing. How did I go from boostin' to wantin' to rob niggas all the time?

I really didn't need the money, I was good for a while. I think it was the rush I felt when we got away with it, I needed to feel it again. It was like an addiction and I would be lying if I said I didn't enjoy what we did. I'm all in now so I hope this girl got another thorough plan.

Tiffany

I was about to head home after leaving Juicy's house, but decided to go see Keyona. I missed her. I had been kind of distant since the baby was born and I knew she was feeling some kind of way about it.

I pulled into her driveway in Shaker Heights. She lived with her grandmother now. It was a huge house that if you were on one side of the house you wouldn't even know someone was on the other side.

She wanted us to get an apartment together, but that would mean I had to take care of Teonna full time and I didn't want that responsibility yet.

I parked on the wrap around driveway and rang the bell. It took about four minutes before she came to the door. When she opened it she flashed her big wide smile at me as if she were surprised to see me. I walked in the corridor and looked around the house before I leaned in and kissed her.

Yes we were a couple now. She was my woman and we were happy being together, but we weren't ready to tell our families that we were living a lesbian life style just yet.

She embraced the kiss and grabbed me by my ass

pulling me closer to her and we were chest to chest. As soon as my body touched hers I immediately became wet. The chemistry was so intense that our breathing picked up as we kissed and I pushed her against the wall.

I began to kiss her neck and she closed her eyes and moaned as I caressed her breast at the same time. I loved her reactions to my touches. Her soft moans made me wetter. I leaned into her ear and softly bit her ear lobe.

"I miss you." I whispered to her.

"I miss you too." She said through her moans.

I slid my right hand into her panties and took my middle finger and slid it inside of her making my finger moist and then back to her clit. She moaned louder.

I started to kiss the other side of her neck as I picked up the pace to make her reach her climax. I knew her body so well. I knew what made her cum. I knew how to make her cum fast too.

I needed to make sure I had her complete attention and she was mine. I owned her right now and I had to be sure she knew that too before I told her about me meeting with Juicy.

I rubbed her clit until I felt her grab me tighter and she squirted all over my hand. I pulled my hand out of her panties and took her juices and rubbed them across her bottom lip, then I reached in and licked it off slowly. Her eyes told me I had her right now, mind body and soul. That's what I wanted. I took my fingers and licked them one by one while she watched.

"You taste good." I said softly.

She blushed.

"Let's go in your room." I said.

"For more?" she sounded excited.

I shook my head. "No, let's go talk."

She looked a little disappointed, but nodded and began to walk to her room while I followed. I wondered if my uncle knew about me and her like he knew everything about Black and them.

I let that thought go quickly and was wondering what I was going to tell Key about working with Juicy or how she would react when I did tell her. I contemplated on finishing what I started with her because the more I had her relaxed the less arguing we would do after I run this by her.

I really wasn't in the mood for sex anyway so I just decided to deal with the possible arguing. I started to take off my shoes then I thought about how things could flip once I told her so I decided to lay across her bed with my legs hanging just in case I had to leave unexpectedly.

Key wasn't stupid by far because when she saw

me do that she leaned against her dresser that was facing me and sucked her teeth as she folded her arms. I knew she picked up on what I was doing, but I wasn't about to start the argument before I talked to her about Juicy so I pretended not to notice her attitude.

"Come 'ere." I said patting the bed next to me. She shook her head.

"Nah, what's up? What you on?" she asked keeping her arms crossed.

I still didn't have the words for her so I said fuck it and let whatever came out just come out.

"I ain't on shyt." I snapped back with a fake attitude to match hers.

"So why haven't I seen you then you come over here like you ready to leave already?"

I took a deep breath as if to let her know that she was irritating me already. She didn't care how I was looking at her, she gave me a look as if to say *hello?*

"What man? I ain't on shyt. I jus' got some shyt to holla at you about and I need you to keep a clear mind."

She let her guards down a little, but didn't move from where she was standing.

"Ok?" I asked.

She sucked her teeth and pouted over to the bed and sat next to me.

"What's up she asked?" still with some irritation in her voice.

"I went to see Juicy." I decided not to even mention my uncle to her at all. She didn't know he was the reason I was even dealing with Black to begin with. I didn't want to tell her about that situation at all. I thought maybe I should have then she would understand why things were going the way they were going.

Her face frowned up. "Fo' what? We agreed we wasn't gonna deal wit' that bitch anymore."

"I need to find Black." I said realizing that I couldn't tell her anything at all about what me and Juicy planned to do.

"For what?" she asked.

I sucked my teeth at her. "For Teonna, why else?"

"Mmm."

'Chill. That's why I didn't even want to tell you about it." I tried to flip it on her.

"Teonna good. She don't need him." She snapped.

I sat up. "You sound stupid as fuck."

She eased back once I sat up. Ever since I beat her ass in my mother's kitchen that one time she never tried me when she saw me get mad.

"Why the fuck wouldn't she need her father?" I asked.

She didn't answer she just shook her head. I got up off the bed. "I'll see you later man."

She jumped up after me and stood in my face. "I'm sorry. Don't go." She said as she hugged me by my waist.

I just stood there waiting for her next move. She leaned in and started to kiss my neck slowly. I relaxed my body and decided to let her kiss my ass for a while.

She started to caress my breast slowly and then went to her knees as she slid my pants down. I looked down at her and smirked. I wondered if this was the feeling niggas got when we did this shyt to them and they knew the head was about to be fire. I let her do what she was going to do and enjoyed every bit of the power I had over her. I think that turned me on more than what she was actually doing to me.

Black

I was packing my Louie Vuitton overnight bag as I felt Aariona stare at me from the bed. I knew I had too much going on right now. She was due soon, I couldn't find my mother and I had to go back to Cleveland.

"What's the plan?" she asked breaking the silence. I didn't give her any eye contact I just kept packing.

"Gotta go to Cleveland." I said.

"When are you going?" she asked.

"As soon as you get ready."

"I'm going?" she asked sounding surprised.

I stopped and looked at her. "Why would I leave you here alone? You are due soon and anything could happen. I can't protect you from Cleveland."

She didn't respond. She just smiled and slid out of bed slowly. I really didn't want to take her but I had no choice. I found her a penthouse suite in Akron to rent out for her. She wouldn't be too close to Cleveland while I did what I had to do and she wouldn't be too far if I needed to get to her for any reason.

I rented the suite for a month. I didn't tell her that because I knew it would start an argument, but I really didn't know what I was going back home to and had to be prepared for whatever.

I started to feel in the pit of my stomach a deep uneasy feeling as I thought about having to go back to Cleveland and about how I couldn't find my mother. I wasn't as worried about her as I was with Aariona. My mother was made for this life; hell if you asked me she was part of the making of the game.

Aariona on the other hand was clueless to how real things really were. All she knew is what she read in street books or seen on hood movies. The closet to how real it can get was when she was tied up in the closet. Every time I even thought about that I hated myself more and found myself getting angrier at each flash back of that day.

Aariona went to the closet and grabbed a bag that was already packed and threw it on the bed. I stopped and raised my eyebrow at her.

"What is that about?"

She smiled. "I wasn't sure if you were taking me or not so I packed my bag last night to be safe."

I smiled and shook my head and continued to pack. "You never cease to amaze me Mrs. Jones."

She sat on the edge of the bed. "Where are we going to stay at when we go?"

"I got you a penthouse suite."

"Me? What you mean you got *me* a penthouse suite?"

I knew this was going to cause an argument and I was already prepared for it. Since we left Cleveland we were inseparable, so I knew she wouldn't be for us separating when we went back home especially with what was going on.

"Don't start." I said trying to see of that would work with her.

"Don't start what Devon?" she snapped back.

"That. Don't start that shyt." I cussed at her for the first time. Not to disrespect her, but to let her know this was not up for debate. "You want me to handle the situation and I'm goin' to." I said reversing it before she could say anything else.

She sucked her teeth and eased up.

"I told you I wanted to be there when you do."

I stopped packing and sat next to her on the bed and looked her in her eyes.

"You speakin' out of emotion right now."

She shook her head. "No, I am speakin' out of hate."

"Emotion." I said again. "This is not like the shyt you read in them books or the movies you watched. This is real. The shyt I've seen and done would make you cry in your sleep."

She jumped up and stood in front of me. "You don't think that shyt that he did to me was real Devon!" she started to yell. I didn't say a word. I let her finish.

"You don't think that shyt makes me cry in my sleep Devon!" she screamed as she pointed her finger in my face and tears started to roll down her cheeks.

The room fell into deep silence and the only sounds were of her crying softly, but never breaking eye contact with me.

"Emotion." Was all I said as I stared back at her.

She became angry when I said it. "Okay, fine, yes, maybe I do have some emotions behind what I want you to do! I'm not a heartless mutha-fucka Devon! He could have killed me and our son!" she reminded me.

I nodded and let her get it out.

"So yes, I am emotional! I almost lost my life and my first child's life; *our* first child!"

"I know. And that is why you will be in the penthouse while I handle my business. Aariona you aren't made for this life."

She sucked her teeth and crossed her arms around and more tears came down her face. I stood up and gently touched her elbows. She made her arms tighter so I couldn't move them. I wanted to comfort her, but not until she understood me and my reasons why I was doing what I was doing.

"This isn't you or for you baby. Trust me." I knew I was going to regret what I was about to say next, but she needed to know what made her so special to me and why I was the way I was with her.

"If you were Juicy and this happened to you I swear I'd be down to ride and have you right next to me and let you even put two in the nigga head yourself."

Her eyes widened and she sucked her teeth and stepped back. I immediately pulled her closer and locked my grip on her elbows.

"But you're not her and that is what I love about you. That is why I married you and not her. She is a fuckin' maggot and that's how she lives. That isn't you and I don't ever want it to be you."

She eased up and stared me in my eyes. I took my right thumb and began to wipe her tears away.

"Don't change. I need you to stay the same woman I fell in love with. I would have never married someone like that. Ever."

It didn't work as smooth as I thought because when she responded I didn't expect what she was going to say. She released the grip I had and threw her arms straight down to her sides pushing me off of her.

"Someone like *you?*" she said as she pierced her eyes at me.

I don't know why, but that actually hurt me. I'm not sure if it was because it was the truth or if it was because it came from her, or possibly both.

"Yeah. Someone like me." I allowed her to hear the hurt in my voice, something I wouldn't ever do with anyone else.

I was okay with being vulnerable with her because even though she was angry with me I knew without a doubt she had my best interest at heart and I knew she wouldn't abuse the privilege.

Her facial expression softened and she looked as if she wanted to apologize, but her pride wouldn't let her.

"You better not ever bring that bitch up to me again, you understand me?" she said as she pointed her finger at me.

I nodded. I knew that was all she had to come back with so I let her have it. I never mentioned Juicy to her at all, but I felt I needed to this time to make my point. She needed to know that she was valuable to me in every way and she was rare and I was in love with rare.

She didn't know what else to say so she wiped both her cheeks at the same time and turned and walked away.

"I'll wait in the car." She said.

I shook my head and went back to packing. I was beginning to regret my lifestyle. It seemed like I was the reason we were having problems. We were so happy until my past showed up; but a big part of me loved my lifestyle.

I actually enjoyed the love I got; the real and the fake. The money and the hood glam; I loved it all. I just wished she understood how much I gave up for her. I know she gave up her whole career for me and for that I was willing to do whatever I had to so that she and I worked.

I glanced over at the clock and saw we spent too much time arguing and started to pack faster. I hurried and zipped my bag and grabbed hers and rushed to the garage.

When I got to the door in the kitchen that led to the garage I dropped my bag to turn off the central air and out of my peripherals I saw a woman standing there and behind her was Aariona.

My heart dropped and I immediately dropped the bag in my left hand. It was my mother. Neither one of us moved. We just locked eyes and stared.

I haven't seen her since that last visit. Only on pictures that she and DJ took on their visits. I couldn't move. It felt as if my feet were cemented to the floor. She had this hard look on her face. I couldn't read her.

She had on some fitted jeans and her hair was pulled straight to the back and she had some grey hair, not much, more like a streak of it on her right side. Her pony tail was to the middle of her back and neat.

She had on a fitted white tank and some sandals. I wasn't curious as to how she got it because my mom left out of prison with a lot of money on her; I made sure she never was low on money or without anything and I still had money waiting to give her.

She had some diamond earring studs in her ears and some nude colored gloss. I could tell she worked out a lot while she was in there. Her arms were so toned and she didn't have a waist or a stomach. She was the most beautiful 45 year old woman I had ever seen.

I didn't even realize I was crying. I was 6'3" and mother was 5'6" so when she walked over to me still staring me in my eyes the whole time and as she got closer she began to look up at me.

She still didn't say anything or even change her facial expression. She just reached up and wiped my face. I couldn't move. I was numb. When she touched my cheeks I closed my eyes because I thought I was dreaming. I had been preparing myself to see her for years, but this was unexpected.

"Hello Son." She said softly as she leaned in and rested her head on my chest.

I pulled her closer to me and hugged her so tight. I looked up and Aariona was still in the doorway. She was crying too as she had both hands in her face in awe over her mouth in the praying position.

There wasn't any movement at all for a long time. I completely forgot all about my flight once I seen her. I just wanted to hug her all day. I prayed for this moment every day for years.

She pulled back. "How are you?"

I didn't answer her I just stared.

"I'm sorry it took me so long to get here. I had some business to handle." She continued.

I was still in awe and couldn't stop staring at her. To see her and hear her voice was unbelievable. I know she told me before to never let this show, but how could anybody hold this in? I felt complete now. Like I could do anything after this.

"Get yourself together. We need to talk." She said.

"I got a flight to catch."

She shook her head. "They can wait. Let's go sit down." She motioned for me to follow her and head nodded to Aariona to do the same.

I looked at Aariona and then followed my mother to the living room. She had been in my house before. When? I couldn't say. She knew her way around too well. She was sneaky so I wasn't surprised.

She went and sat on the couch that faces the window and rested her elbows on her knees as she stared out the window.

Aariona wobbled behind me and sat in her recliner. I sat next to my mother.

"Where were you?" I had to ask.

She glanced at Aariona then back at me then looked out the window again.

"C'mon on, Son. You know better." She said soflty.

I looked at Aariona then immediately at my mother.

"This is my *wife,* Ma, not a girl friend or some broad I'm smashin', but my wife." I said letting her know I trusted Aariona.

"Oh yeah? If it's so deep, why the *fuck* didn't you put a bullet in Bishop's head when he came here and tied her up?" she yelled at me as she pointed her finger at my face.

I dropped my head in shame. I could take Aariona

yelling at me about it because I knew I was going to kill Bishop; but disappointing my mother, I couldn't handle.

She shook her head at me. "Jus' as I thought. You always had a soft side for that faggot."

My eyes widened. How much did she know about the outside while she was inside? And how long had she really been free.

"Have I not taught you *anything* at all?" she asked.

"How do you know all this?" I became skeptical of her altogether. Normally I would be impressed, but this *is* the same person who has always told me trust nobody and she was the one person I trusted completely.

"I know everything." She said. "I'm God." She didn't crack a smile; her face stayed the same.

Aariona sat up straight in the recliner as if she was fascinated and very much intrigued with my mother. I saw it all over her face and at that moment I wanted her to leave the room. I could see that was her way in to this life that she was so fascinated by and I know my mother would have no problem at all teaching her the game. That is something I didn't want.

I stood up. "Give me and my mother a minute." I said waving Aariona out the room.

She shook her head. "No, I am your wife remember? We are family now and this is a family matter." She looked over to my mother for her to agree.

I looked down at my mother and she smirked, but didn't say a word. I became irritated immediately. One thing I wouldn't tolerate was two women coming at me in my house.

"Man, get the fuck on wit' that." I snapped using my thumb to point behind me telling her once again to leave the room.

She knew I was serious the way I responded and sucked her teeth and stood up. "I can't believe you." She said shaking her head.

"Believe it." I snapped back as I watched her stomp out the room like a toddler having a tantrum that I didn't give a fuck about.

My mother nodded her head in approval. "I was hopin' that is how you handled that."

I just stared at her. She stood up. "Let's go out in the back and talk. We need some fresh air."

I followed her as if this were her house. I really just wanted to watch and see how she walked around here because it still blew me that she knew my house so well.

As we walked through my backyard I didn't say anything and neither did she. She just stared off at the landscape of the yard and kind of smiled at everything to herself. I could tell she was just enjoying the moment and her freedom so I gave her that time in silence.

"This is beautiful. I'm proud of you." She said stopping in her tracks and giving me eye contact.

"Thank you."

"Where did you find her?" she asked nodding her head toward the house without losing eye contact.

"I met her a few years back at a gas station."

"You never mentioned her to me."

I shrugged. "We were jus' friends then."

"Careful of that word, Son. You - have – *no* – friends."

"She is my friend." I said not bending on that one.

"Mmm. And you are sure of this?" she asked nitpicking.

I nodded. "Positive."

"Just as sure as you were about DJ?" she continued.

I could feel my anger slowly rising. I still wasn't over the fact DJ wasn't my son. I missed that kid and I knew he missed me too. Our bond was real.

"So who kid is she havin'? she continued to pick. This time I could tell she knew she was getting to me because she had a smirk on her face. "Huh?"

"Mine." I said confidently. "You knew DJ wasn't mine huh?"

She nodded. "Just like I know that one ain't yours

either."

Now I felt like she was reaching and reaching hard. *I* took Aariona virginity. *I* made sure *I* planted my seed and *I* made *sure* this one was mine for sure.

I laughed at her. For the first time in my life I was looking at my own mother sideways. I was disappointed in her this time.

"Chill, G. That's my kid." I said attempting to end this convo and get to the real business.

She didn't like how I responded and slid both her hands in her back pockets of her jeans and stared at me.

"Unless God himself blessed your dick with new sperm, that ain't your child. You can't have any kids. I was told when you were younger by your doctor that you were sterile."

I stopped smiling. Is she serious? Can they really tell that when you're that young or is she just on some real bull shyt right now?

"Stop playin' Ma. I buss all the time, I *know* I got sperm."

"Yeah, you got it, but the shyt don't work. So I don't know who got Ms. Perfect pregnant, but it ain't you. Maybe Bishop faggot ass got her too." She said laughing.

"That's funny to you?" I snapped. 'You wait all

these years to tell me I can't have kids and you wait until now, right before my son is born?"

She shrugged. "From jail never seemed like the right place to tell you."

"What about all them fuckin' visits I had with you prior to you endin' them? At some point you should have told me!" I yelled.

She kept a smirk on her face and didn't say anything as I yelled at her.

"You're lyin'."

She shrugged again. "Okay."

Silence fell on us and we had a staring match.

"I have to go see if I can get a new flight since I missed mine."

She nodded.

"Are you staying here?"

"Nah. I have some business in Cleveland myself."

"You want me to book your flight too?"

She shook her head. "Nah. I already did."

I turned to walk back toward the house.

Son, when you kill Bishop, don't do it for her. Do it for you. Do it because he disrespected you on so many levels. Remember all that he has done to you. If she wanted him dead for what he did to her, let her kill him herself."

"She's not like that, Ma. I can handle shyt he's done to me, but I'll never let him or anyone else hurt her or you." I said still believing and trusting in my wife.

"Hmmm." She said.

"Not everyone is as fucked up as us, Ma. When all this shyt over Imma introduce you to some good people."

I felt so bad for her. She really believed that everyone is out to get you. I remember when I believed that too; until Aariona showed me something different. I walked back to her and kissed her forehead and then back toward the house.

I knew Aariona well, she didn't, but it didn't stop me from wondering if I was really sterile and couldn't make babies. She has never given me a reason to distrust her; never until my mother said that to me. Now it was one more thing I needed to deal with.

Juicy

"So you really not goin' to respond to my mama letters, Juicy?" Bishop asked as he followed me around my house while I was cleaning.

"Fo' what?" I asked never making any eye contact.

I stopped and grabbed a rubber band off of the table and tied my hair up as I looked in my mirror that was over the dinette set. When I glanced at him standing behind me he was staring at my butt which made me immediately turn around to break his stare. I knew that my tank and booty shorts looked sexy on me, but I assumed he was over women since him and Juvey been fuckin'.

He looked directly at me. "What the fuck you mean fo' what? She ain't did shyt to you. That was yo' girl a few months ago, she get locked up and you get ghost? That's fucked up. You wasn't like that wit' Peaches."

I really didn't give a fuck about what he was talking about right now. I knew he was trying to start an argument when he brought up Black's mama. I really had my mind on why I haven't heard from Tae in a few days and what I was going to wear to the Prive tonight. I gave him a *I don't give a fuck* look as I leaned against my dining room table and rested my hands on it to prop me up.

I shrugged. "Ask Juvey to write her." That slipped out. He still didn't know that I knew about them.

His face dropped and he looked as if he wanted to ask me what I heard.

"What's that supposed to mean?" he asked anyway.

I tried to clean it up fast. "I-I jus' meant since his ass always wanna do shyt for you….never mind." I couldn't come up with anything fast enough.

He nodded. "Yeah, ok. Stalyce need us right now. The lawyer say she comin' home tho'."

I frowned. "How?"

He shrugged. "I don't know. I'm jus' makin' sure the lawyer is paid on time."

"Mmm." I said as I gave him a sideway look and pierced my lips and folded my arms.

"Nah, nah it ain't even what you think." He said waving his hands as if to say no. "She ain't never been no snitch. You know she solid."

"Whatever, I hope not. She know better."

He got closer to me. "What's up?"

I sucked my teeth. "Ain't shyt up." I said as I pushed him back.

Bishop hated rejection of any sort. "Come here."

Months ago this would have turned me on and I would have been on my knees deep throating him savoring the taste, but now I was disgusted and wondered if his dick was infected. The thought gave me a bad taste in my mouth.

"I'm good." I said backing up.

He stared at me like he wanted to cuss me out. "Who you fuckin'?"

I laughed. "It's been months and *now* you wanna know who I'm fuckin'?" I shook my head.

He kept the same look and never blinked or said a word. He waited for me to answer.

"That's none of your business."

He gave a laugh to him self as he shook his head and moved closer to me. I used to be afraid of him the last time he did that to me when we were standing in Dj's room at the hospital, but after the robbery I wasn't afraid of him at all.

"If you have the nigga around my son Imma kill you *and* him."

I honestly tried my hardest not to laugh, but it snuck up out of me. All I could think about is how I stomped his ass out in the kitchen and all this fake ass gangster shyt that he was giving me now had absolutely no effect on me.

"Yeah….ok." I said still laughing at him." I began to walk away when he grabbed me by my throat and pulled me back to him.

I immediately became defensive and took my left hand and punched him in his jaw as I tried to release his grip on my throat. I could tell the hit took him by surprise by the way his brows frowned up at me and he squeezed tighter.

"Get the fuck off me!" I yelled as I used both hands to punch him.

Even though I was fighting back he was still stronger than I was. As he squeezed tighter as if he was trying to make me pass out I began to kick as hard as I could while still punching him with both hands. He maneuvered his hips in between my thighs as he lifted me off the floor and threw me on top of the table. He never released his grip and I could feel myself getting light headed as tear started to run down my cheeks.

"Please stop." I begged through short breaths.

I almost wished I didn't because he gave a smirk as if he was enjoying this moment. He released his right hand, but made his left one tight around my entire neck. He took his free hand and slid them down between my legs. I started to scream and he squeezed some more.

"Bishop, stop. Please." I said between tears.

He leaned in and slid his tongue in my mouth as he ripped my shorts pulling them to the side. I closed my eyes and let the tears fall. I knew he was enjoying this too much and I tried to make my mind go elsewhere.

"This my pussy." He whispered as he slid his fingers inside me and began to massage my clit with his thumb.

I felt so humiliated and terrified by what he was doing, but my body was being turned on because he knew my spots. I started to cry more in hopes he would stop seeing how he was hurting me.

He took his hand out of me and pulled his dick out of his joggers and slid inside me with a hard thrust. My pussy loved it because he warmed me up, but I hated every second of it. I was being raped by the father of my child and the tears flowed as if someone died.

"See how wet she get for Daddy?" he whispered as he finally let my neck go and pulled me by my ass closer to him.

I continued to cry and tried to push him out of me, but his grip was too much. "Please." I whispered through tears.

He ripped the top of my tank and pulled out my breast and began to lick my nipples. "Mmmm." He said as he sucked them one by one.

I kept pushing him, but he used his body weight to control the situation. I got weak from fighting him and started to give up. He pushed my back against the table so I could lay flat and I turned my head to the right and stared at the wall.

I stopped crying and zoned out and tried to pretend I wasn't there. He was just using my body is what I tried to convince myself. I started to replay the day I stomped his face in, but this time picturing myself actually putting a bullet in his head when it was over.

He was enjoying this moment too much and he held me by my hips and kept pumping. He pulled out and I looked at him in hopes he was done, but instead he took his right hand and started to jack off until he began to cum all over my thighs and my pussy.

I felt contaminated and nasty. I felt as though not even a shower could make me feel clean after this. My body felt numb and I didn't move. I actually prayed that he would just kill me now because if he didn't kill me, I was definitely going to kill him. He smirked as he used the ripped piece of my tank to clean himself off. He leaned in and took the tip of his tongue and licked my clit and out of natural reaction my body jerked and he laughed and then kissed it softly and stood straight back up and locked eyes with me.

"That's my shyt."

I never responded.

He tapped the outside of my left thigh. "Go clean yourself up."

I sat straight up on the table. I was numb from the inside out and my neck was hurting. My face was still wet from all the crying I was doing which seemed to turn this sick fuckin' faggot on.

He leaned in and kissed my cheek. I closed my eyes when his lips touched my skin.

"You raped me." I whispered.

He laughed as he stepped back. "I raped you?"

I nodded slowly, never looking directly at him but from the corners of my left eye where he was still standing.

He smiled and took a slow step back. "Juicy, you belong to me. How can I rape what's mine?"

I knew that he had lost his mind for sure. I didn't know this man in front of me at all.

"Write my mother back." He went back to that as if nothing just happened.

I closed my eyes and took my right arm and covered my breast with it as I locked onto my left arm. I didn't feel the confident, sexy woman I always felt when a man is looking at me while I was naked. Instead I felt cheap and dirty.

Bishop turned and left the house. I eased off the table. My body was sore already so I could only imagine how I would feel later. I didn't even bother to lock the door because nothing mattered anymore at this point. I went to the shower with my clothes still on me and turned the shower to cold and stepped in slowly.

The water ran over my face as I closed my eyes then slowly sat down on the floor of the shower. I pulled my knees to my chest and held them tightly. I wanted to cry, but I couldn't. There wasn't a single tear that would come out anymore.

I wanted to call on God, but I didn't know Him well enough to keep praying to someone I really wasn't sure if He existed. If he was real I couldn't see Him allowing so much bull shyt to keep happening to me since I was born.

I couldn't take the way I felt and I only wanted to kill him. Not just shoot and kill, but actually make him feel pain; almost torture him and then kill him.

As the water continued to run on me I realized that the only way I could kill him and get away with it is as if I asked for help and the only person I knew could get away with it is Tiffany.

I wasn't going to go to the Prive after what just happened, but I knew I had to talk to her right away so I stood up and pulled my clothes off and began to scrub my body.

I turned to the water as hot as I could stand it. I scrubbed my body until my skin was raw and red. No matter how hard I scrubbed I still felt nasty.

When I got out of the shower I wrapped the towel around me and sat on the edge of the tub. I couldn't hold in the tears any longer and began to scream and cry louder and louder until I found myself lying on the floor in the fetal position.

I never imagined my life to have taken the turns it has taken this past year and I wished I could rewind time. I felt hopeless and lost. I wondered what other women who were raped felt and what they did to stay strong.

I closed my eyes and hoped it was a nightmare I was going to awake from soon. I knew in reality it was real until I dozed off right there on the floor.

Tiffany

I was blowing Juicy phone up to make sure that we were still on for tonight because it was no way in hell I was going to East Cleveland without seeing someone I knew. I've heard many stories about that side of town and even though I wasn't afraid, I wasn't dumb either.

I felt like something was wrong because when I was at her house she seemed like she was down for what we planned to do so her not answering my text or phone calls did seem out of the norm.

I decided to go over to her house to make sure she was cool. As I was throwing on a tank and leggings my mother walked in my room with Teonna on her hip.

"You can't keep leavin' this baby like you do, Tiff." She began in on her lecture.

I rolled my eyes as I looked for my tennis shoes. I was going for my flip flops, but decided against it just in case my gut feeling that something was wrong was true.

"Tiffany!" she yelled so that I would look at her.

"What!" I yelled back as I sat on the bed to put my shoes on.

"Are you listening to me?"

"I hear you."

"I said listening, not hear. It's bad enough the girl

don't have a father now she don't have a mother too?"

"Really? You bring that up?" I gave her an evil stare.

"You are this girl's mother and you act like she belong to me!"

I stood up. "Well that's what you did with my brothers. I took care of them, so I guess we even."

She closed her mouth and pulled Teonna closer to her. I smirked and walked past her and out the house. I didn't feel bad at all for what I said because it was the truth. I agreed with her not having her father and she needed him and that is why I really wanted to find Black, not for my uncle, but for her to be able to go live with him in Miami or wherever he really may be at.

I pulled up at Juicy's house and parked a house over so that I could see if I saw any sign that something was wrong. The sun was going down and I could see right through her picture window of her house.

Her 2012 red Audi car was parked in the driveway and I didn't see any other car so I assumed she was in there alone or with her son. I called her phone again as I stared at the window to see if I saw any movement, but this time the phone went to voicemail.

That was strange to me so I got out of my car and walked to the house. Her front door was closed so as I walked to the side of the house; I looked around to make sure no one saw me go to her house and headed to knock on the door.

Her car didn't look like it had been messed with, but the side door was open. Not wide open, but enough to push it open. I felt my heart pound slightly and wished I hadn't have left my gun in the car. I went ahead in anyway because I didn't think I would really need it if something was wrong. Part of me felt like whatever was wrong already has happened so I didn't really need my gun.

I slowly walked inside the house stepping up the steps that led through her kitchen.

"Juicy?" I called out.

No answer.

I continued to walk around her dimly lit house looking for her. I glanced in her son room and he wasn't there so I continued down her hallway and called her name again.

"Juicy!" I said a little louder.

I heard some groans and I paused to make sure I was hearing right. I stepped back toward the bathroom and saw her laying on the floor. My heart stopped for a second.

"Juicy?"

She looked up at me and her eyes were swollen as if she had been crying. I kneeled down next to her.

"Are you okay?"

She sat up and stared at me, but didn't say a word. Her face was so puffy and I could see marks on her neck.

"What happened?"

As soon as I said that she burst into tears and laid her head on me crying loudly and saying "oh God" over and over. I sat completely on the floor then and held her as she cried. I wasn't sure what happened to her, but I felt bad for her. I've never seen her so vulnerable and the fact she let me see it of all people tells me something bad went down. I just hoped it had nothing to do with her son again.

I let her cry a little longer then I pulled her up. "C'mon."

"What made you come over here?" she finally asked.

I shrugged. "I was calling you and somethin' told me somethin' wasn't right because I haven't heard from you."

I grabbed a wash cloth and soaked it in cold water. She sat on the toilet and just stared off. I watched her from the corner of my eyes as I wrung the rag out to put on her face then sat on the edge of the tub in front of her.

"What happened?"

"What time we goin' to the Prive?" she asked ignoring my question.

I shook my head. "You no goin' to the Prive. I really need to know what happened cause you might not even be stayin' here tonight."

She stared me directly in my eyes. "Bishop raped me."

I dropped my head. I could only imagine how she felt right now especially being raped by him. He been out here jus' raw doggin' niggas in the booty ain't no tellin' what his ass done picked up.

I wasn't a sentimental woman at all and if I had any ounce of it in me ever it was definitely dead. So asking how she felt was out of the question.

"What you wanna do?" I asked.

I take it that's what she wanted to hear because her face lit up.

"I want to kill him."

"Okay. Let's kill him then. The Prive can wait." I said.

"You serious?" she asked desperately.

I nodded. I liked Juicy, I would never admit that to her, but she was a cool as female to me and even though I would make it to Keyona like I would kill her or fuck her over to keep peace with my girl, I really wouldn't. Plus I didn't give a fuck about Bishop so killing him wasn't nothin' to me.

"Have you ever killed someone?" she asked.

She knew the answer to that already so I knew this was a trick question.

"I had never robbed anyone before, but look how that turned out when I did?"

She laughed a little then stopped and immediately grabbed her neck.

I shook my head. "You couldn't have thought you was gon pull a prospect tonight lookin' like Pacquiao after a few rounds wit' Mayweather."

She laughed, "Shuttup. I don't look that bad."

I widened my eyes as I lifted my eyebrows at the same time. "Okay."

She stood up and tightened her towel as she looked in the mirror. She touched her neck softly and then her eyes. She started to cry again and I stood up to stop her before she started.

"Chill. That cryin' shyt is over wit'. We gon get his ass."

She nodded. "I jus' can't believe he did this to me."

"Why can't you? Nothin' should surprise you

anymore."

"You right."

"Now get yourself together. It's gon' take me a minute to come up wit' somethin' for him. As far as the Prive, we can jus' go next week when you back to normal."

"Okay."

I started to walk back to the way I came in with her following me. She turned on lights as we walked because the house was dark.

"Oh and charge your phone. I called and it went to voicemail."

"Okay. Tiff?"

I stopped and turned toward her. "Yeah?"

"Thank you for checkin' on me." She leaned in and hugged me.

I hugged her back, but didn't respond.

"Call me when you get up tomorrow." I headed down the steps and when I opened the door my Uncle was standing there.

I immediately became nervous at the fact he followed me to her house. You could see it all over my face that I was scared, but his remained calm.

I couldn't believe he was that desperate to find Black that he followed me to Juicy house. I looked behind me at Juicy on my heels and my first instinct was to push her back inside the house and close the door.

"Hey Baby." She said before I could push her back.

Baby?

"What's up." He said dryly as he reached past me to hug her.

Baby? I was completely lost now.

She paused for a second then she introduced us. "This my cousin Tiffany." She lied.

He laughed slightly and gave a smile. "What's up?"

His smile had so much deceit behind it and I was impressed. He was so calm and to anyone who didn't know, just like Juicy doesn't know, he was able to pull it off as if we were complete strangers. I relaxed my face to match his. After all we were from the same blood line and disappointing him right now I didn't want to do.

"You look familiar." He said. "Kind of like my niece."

"I get that a lot." I said meeting his eye contact.

Juicy didn't say a word. I don't know why, but deep down I wanted to be on her team. I wanted to warn her and tell her who he was to me, but I couldn't; not right now at least.

"I gotta go, Cuz." I said to her. "You cool?"

She nodded. "I'm good."

I nodded back.

My Uncle moved to the side opening the storm door for me as I walked through. I didn't say bye and neither did he. He just walked in the house and closed the door.

As I walked across the street to my car I noticed he wasn't driving his usual BMW, this time he was in his royal blue Cadillac CTS. He rarely drove that car so I knew he was on some real bull shyt.

I hopped in my car and sat parked for a minute to think about what just happened. I knew first hand he was up to something because he definitely knew who she was so his interest in her was pure bull shyt. I don't think I have ever seen him with a woman before on a serious note.

Then Juicy just called him *Baby* which tells me that he has been around her for a while now. At least since the robbery because she was with Bishop then. It was something going on and I was going to find out one way or another. I couldn't have my uncle messing with my business with her.

Black

We stepped off the plane in Akron and my stomached bubbled. Aariona didn't say a word to me all the way here and I was okay with that because I need to gather my thoughts about everything that was going on now. I never wanted to have my wife mad at me for anything, but she and I were forever so I would make it up to her later.

I didn't believe my mother telling me I was sterile. I figured she was just on some bull shyt and that's why she said what she said. I didn't know her anymore. I wasn't the same boy she left years ago.

I was a man now and even though I respected her and the thing's she taught me growing up, I was still capable of making my own choices and I *know* Aariona wouldn't do anything to hurt me.

I just couldn't see what my mother was trying to do by telling me that. I also couldn't see what would make her get out of jail and not tell me of all people. I was the one that was taking care of her the whole time so I thought she and I were better than that.

"Devon." Aariona said breaking the silence as I put our bags in the trunk of the rental.

"Yeah." I answered hoping she wasn't about to

start no shyt again.

"I don't wanna stay in the hotel alone."

I didn't respond I just closed the trunk and walked to her side of the car and opened her door for her. She stood there staring at me with her arms folded and I just stared back while I held onto the passenger door with my right hand.

She sucked her teeth and pouted some more.

"What you want me to say, Aariona?"

"I don't know. Say something!"

"We don't have time for this."

"Are you serious?" she shouted.

I looked around the airport. A few people stopped and looked while others carried on with their business.

I took a deep breath. "I didn't expect this from you."

"What!" She yelled as she walked closer to me.

"I said I didn't expect this from you. You changin'."

Her eyes got wider and her mouth dropped. "You don't think that all the shyt that's goin' on would have some kind of change in me?" she yelled as she pointed her finger in my face.

I backed up some because I could feel myself getting angry and I didn't want to disrespect my wife, but she was getting out of control.

"Chill Aariona and watch your mouth."

"Watch my mouth?" she stepped closer.

This wasn't a side I ever thought I would see from her and I was feeling a flash back of the women I used to deal with.

"Aariona, get in the car." I sounded as serious as I could to let her know I was done arguing.

She closed her mouth and got in the car. I closed her door and walked to my side of the car.

Before she could start in again I looked her in her eyes and I began to talk over her. "I knew that this shyt could change you, but don't let it. I told you I would handle it and I will. I can't do it with you stressin' me tho'."

She dropped her head. "But-"

I cut her off. "Be my peace of mind ok? A nigga got enough to worry about out here. I don't need my woman" she immediately looked up at me and I corrected myself, "my wife. I don't need my wife stressin' me too."

I hoped that this kept her cool for at least until I was done handling my business.

"Ok." She said quietly.

I took a sigh of relief and leaned back in my seat. I

took my right hand and massaged the back of her head as I drove to the hotel. I was hoping that the attitude was from her being pregnant as well as what was going on because as long as I have known her she has never cussed the way she does now or yell.

I began to wonder if I was changing her into something she wasn't. I wondered if I was draining her of all the good that was in her and she was slowly becoming like me. I feared that thought because I knew it would be over for us if that was the case.

Her mood changed when we walked into the hotel. She was smiling when the front desk began to treat us as royalty.

"Good evening Mr. Jones, I hope that you and your lovely wife enjoy your stay this month."

I dropped my head when he said that because I saw Aariona's smile immediately disappear and her eyes landed directly on me.

"Thank you." I said looking directly at him as I took the key to the room.

We stepped onto the elevator and she was ready to say something then to me, but there was people already on there. I pushed the elevator to go to the penthouse. The older couple that was already on there was staring at us and smiling. I smiled back while

Aariona kept her frown. I knew then it was going to be a long night.

"When are you due, Honey?" the elderly woman asked her.

She ignored her.

"In a few weeks." I told the lady.

She stared at Aariona and I could tell she was wondering why she didn't answer herself. She looked down at her hand then at her husband.

"How long have you two been married?" she asked me this time.

"Six months."

She and her husband looked at each other and laughed.

"First child?"

I nodded and the elevator opened and her husband stepped off first. She leaned into Aariona and touched her arm lightly.

"Let it go Hunny. You have so much more to be mad at your husband about for many years to come. Right now enjoy each other and the new baby to come."

Aariona didn't say anything back to her she just looked at her as she exited the elevator and the doors shut. I hoped that would change her mood.

She looked at me and then moved closer to me

and grabbed me and hugged me tight as she buried her head in my chest.

"You should have told me. You starting to keep things from me. You the one changing."

I hugged her back. She was right. I was keeping things from her, but not because I don't trust her, but because I was trying to protect her. The less she knew the better.

"I'm sorry."

The elevator doors opened and we both stepped out not saying anything to each other after that.

The suite was so nice I knew that she wouldn't mind staying here for a month, if we really had to stay for a month.

She kicked her shoes off and went straight to the couch and propped her feet up on the coffee table.

"What's the deal with your mom?"

I knew eventually she and I had to talk about her and I really didn't want to, but I had to.

"What you mean?" I asked to be sure before I gave more information than I had to.

"Why didn't she tell you she was out? I mean I'm not saying anything about your mother but-"

"Then don't." I stopped her before she said something to make me snap.

"I wasn't done talking." She said sternly.

"Yes you were. Order whatever you want for dinner. I'm headed to Cleveland to get this shyt over wit'. Don't call me unless it's important. I'll be back."

I kissed her forehead and walked out before she could say anything else. I love my wife more than anything, but I won't let her get used to saying whatever the fuck she felt like saying to me or about my mother.

I couldn't lie to myself as the elevator was taking me down to the lobby; it was going to feel good to hit those streets in Cleveland. No matter where you go in the world; there's no place like home.

Juicy

I walked to my room and quickly threw on a t-shirt and jogging pants and attempted to act normal now that Tae was here. I wasn't sure if I wanted to tell him about what happened with Bishop, but I couldn't think of a way to explain my puffy eyes or marks on my neck.

He followed behind me and took off his clothes and got in the bed. I tied my hair up and was hoping he didn't want to have sex. I knew that would be impossible for me tonight.

"Where you been?" I asked breaking the silence.

"Workin'."

I didn't know what else to say. From his response I could tell he didn't feel like being questioned and I honestly didn't care to anyway. My mind was replaying the things from earlier and how Tiffany came by to check on me.

Then it dawned on me that Tiffany and Tae knew each other by the way they interacted and so I decided to pick at that for a little while.

"How do you know my lil' cousin?"

"Who?"

I could tell he asked that to buy him some time to think of a lie. I sat next to him on the bed and crossed my legs.

"Tiffany." I let him have it.

"I don't."

I smirked. "I can tell by the way y'all looked at each other that you do. And I can also tell that neither one of you knew that you both knew me. So how do you know her?"

No response. Just a blank stare.

"You fucked her?"

Still no answer.

"You fucked her?" I asked again, this time with some emotions behind the question.

"No, Juicy. I never fucked her."

I calmed myself. "So where you know her from?"

"I don't. What happened to your neck?" he asked changing the subject and sitting up straight to get a closer look.

I didn't respond this time.

"Juicy, what the fuck happened to your neck."

"I got into a fight."

"With?"

"Bishop."

"About?"

I could tell my one word responses were beginning to agitate him.

"Some bull shyt. Everything cool. I handled it." I lied. I really didn't want him to get involved because I wanted to get my own revenge.

"Looks like he handled you. Where this nigga be at?"

I knew that was coming. I loved that he wanted to protect me, but I really needed him to let me handle this one.

"Babe, it's okay." I leaned in and kissed him. "Can we jus' go to bed I'm really tired right now."

He rolled his eyes and lay back on his pillow. "Ok."

I laid on his chest and scooted as close to him as I could. I needed to feel protected and secure right now. I was glad he came by because I didn't want to be alone right now.

He reached over and turned the night light off and I heard him snoring within ten minutes. I couldn't sleep. I began to replay how Bishop turned into a monster out of nowhere and I tried to block it out.

The more I replayed the day moment for moment I wondered how Tiffany really knew Tae. She didn't look afraid that a man was standing at the door; it was more so that it was a shocker that someone she knew was there.

Then I wondered if me meeting him was on purpose and that's why he was so persistent when he was trying to talk to me.

I rolled off of him slowly and laid on my back and looked at the ceiling. Things were starting to seem fishy the more I thought about it and I know first-hand what Tiffany is capable of doing.

I can't figure out what they could be up to when it came to me though. I thought about just asking Tiffany myself. She said for me to call her when I woke up and that's exactly what I planned on doing.

Tae interrupted my thoughts when he woke up and rolled over and put his arms around me and pulled me closer to him. I arched my back and slid my butt closer to his pelvis and cuffed his arms tighter around me. I closed my eyes and lay there until I finally fell asleep.

Black

I rented a white Altima so that I wouldn't be noticed right away while I was in Cleveland. People weren't used to see me driving anything like this so I wouldn't alert anyone right away as I drove through the hood.

My first stop I got off on 55th and drove by The Marathon. It was a nice day in Cleveland. It felt good to be home. I didn't miss the bull shyt, but I definitely missed home.

I made a left and decided to go up Kinsman toward The Valley. It was just habit for me to go that way and part of me did hope that I ran into Juicy so I could see DJ.

In my heart he was still my son. I tried to let him go, but it was hard. I wondered everyday how he was after he got shot and if Bishop was treating him right. I hoped he kept that faggot shyt away from him.

As I came closer to the Valley I didn't even recognize it. There were new town homes in the place of the projects that were there forever. I made a right and the playground that we kicked it at was gone. I continued to drive up the street and noticed the other projects were in the process of being torn down.

I hadn't been gone that long and already everything was different. I drove around the building that Juicy lived in and it was empty too. I parked the car and just stared for a minute, sort of reminiscing on my time there. I didn't miss being here too much, but I missed the memories and good times.

A knock on the window broke my thoughts and caught me sort of off guard. I looked up as I slowly reached for my gun. It was Dude. I laid my gun in my lap and rolled the window down.

"Yo, man I thought that was you!" he sounded excited as he reached his hand in my window to dap me up.

I cringed in the inside. "What up?"

"You back?" he asked.

Him asking was I back let me know that he knew I was gone which means he still dealt with Bishop. I nodded.

"Briefly."

He smirked and nodded. "That's what's up."

I didn't like this nigga. I wish he hadn't seen me just now because I wasn't ready for Bishop to know I was back yet. I needed to check out the scenery before I made my presence known, but since he did I have to play the cards I'm dealt right now.

"Lookin' fo' Juicy?" he asked.

I squinted my eyes at him. "What the fuck you talkin' bout yo'?"

He stood up straight and backed away a step.

"I jus' thought since you was in the Valley you was lookin' fo' her."

I shook my head. "Nah. I jus' was lookin' at my old home."

He looked toward where she used to live then back at me. "She live in Maple now."

I shrugged.

"You want her number?"

He was just like a female too; grillin' me wit' questions. I did want her number so that I could see DJ, but I didn't want it to backfire on me so I shook my head.

He sucked his teeth. I looked at him a little closer. Bishop face was fucked up and now I noticed a gash across his face.

"Yo' what the fuck happened to you?"

He shook his head a looked away.

"You and Bishop face fucked up, what happened to y'all niggas man?" I wouldn't let up.

"Nigga, you know what the fuck happened." He snapped.

I raised my eyebrow. This nigga must have forgot

who I was the way he just responded so I hopped out the car to remind him. I slammed the door behind me and crossed my arms with my gun in my right hand and had it where he could still see it, but let it rest by my side.

He looked nervous and relaxed his attitude a bit. I loved it. I gave him a side way smirk. I know that when he saw my size he was nervous just from that.

I had been in the gym heavy and I had on a black wife beater that showed the definition in my arms and chest clear.

"Before you left, some niggas robbed us." He started talking without me having to repeat myself.

This is the shyt I missed. Being able to bring the bitch out of these niggas with just my presence.

"Why wasn't you at the meetin' man?"

It was starting to make sense now.

"So you think because I wasn't there it was *me*?"

He didn't respond. He just stared.

"Nigga you should know better than that. If it was me that robbed y'all niggas I would have killed you before I left."

He looked down for a second and nodded.

"You right. That's what Bishop said too. That he don't believe it was you."

I leaned back against the car and looked around to

see if anyone else was out.

"Where is Bishop?"

He shrugged. "Last I heard from him he was on Hayden."

I looked puzzled. "Hayden?"

He nodded.

"Why would he be across town?"

"Business."

"With who?" I asked still not connecting the pieces.

He shrugged.

"Ain't shyt on Hayden tho'." I said still confused.

We only had one stash house over that way and that was on Superior. That was the house that we were supposed to have the meeting at, but I never went to because Tiffany told me she overheard them saying that they planned to kill me.

I looked down and laughed as it dawned on me what she did. That devious bitch. She was the one that set them up. She made me get out of dodge so her plan could fall through. I smiled at the idea.

But how could she have pulled that off and with who? That's what I needed to find out.

"Who was there when the house got robbed?" I asked to start my own investigation.

"Me, Bishop, Stalyce and Juvey."

My first mind would have been that Juvey helped her set it up, but she wasn't fuckin' with him after she found out he was a fag too.

"How many niggas robbed y'all?"

"Three. "

"And you sure it was niggas?" I asked to be clear.

He nodded with a confused look on his face.

That's the part that was throwing me off. She wasn't a female that hung around niggas. She didn't even have many friends except Keyona. My mind couldn't even picture who she could have had pull this shyt off.

"Hmmm."

"What?" he eagerly asked.

I gave him a look as if to say get the fuck out my face.

"Let me check somethin' out." I said as I hopped back in my car.

"Aye, want me go with you?"

I frowned at him. I hope this faggot didn't think I was one of them. I shook my head. "Nah, but I think I do need Juicy number and address. I pulled out my phone so that I could take the information down.

Once he gave it to me I locked it in and tucked my gun. "Don't tell Bishop I'm here yet. It might fuck up what I got goin'."

He nodded.

I didn't trust that he would keep it on the low that I was here, but I still said it anyway.

I turned around and went back up Kinsman and headed towards where Tiffany lived. I thought about going to see Juicy first, but I was closer to Tiffany's house.

I turned on her street off Miles and saw my mother coming from her house. I parked my car a few houses down and slouched down and watched.

What the hell was she doing there? And how did she even know about Tiffany or even know her? My mother looked around just as she always have checking her surroundings, she stared in my direction briefly and I slouched down even further. She paused and then got in her car and pulled off.

I sat up straight as I watched Tiffany come out the house and head toward a white Altima similar to the rental I was in. I started to pull off fast behind her when my cell phone rang.

"Yeah?" I answered never checking the caller ID because I assumed it was Aariona calling me as I trailed behind Tiffany.

"Don't follow her. Meet me at the bookstore in Beachwood by Red Lobster.

"The book store?" I frowned my face as I still

followed Tiffany.

"What you up to, Ma?"

"Do what I said." She snapped and disconnected the call.

As bad as I wanted to follow Tiffany right now I decided to meet my mother instead. Things weren't adding up right now and I had to get to the bottom of it fast.

I walked in Barnes and Noble Bookstore about 20 minutes after I hung up with my mother. She was sitting at the Starbucks drinking coffee by the time I got to her. She was facing the window and had the same look that she had when I first saw her that was hard to read.

I sat across from her so I could look her in her eyes. As much as I hated the thought, but I felt like she came home untrustworthy too.

"Hey, Son."

I didn't say anything. I crossed my hands in front of me on the table and looked her in her eyes.

"Its things going on I can't tell you about right now." She said.

"You need to say something. I'm not a little boy anymore. I'm a grown ass man."

She smiled. The first real smile she gave since she came home.

"No, you're not a boy anymore. I know." She said as she placed her right hand on my cheek. "But you are still my son and I still have to protect you."

"From what?" I was confused. "What do you know, Ma?"

"Didn't I teach you that when you learn somethin' never reveal it?"

I sucked my teeth and waved my left hand. "Man, fuck all that shyt right now. You caught a flight, I caught a flight and I see you comin' out of my old bitch house? Yo' man what was that about?"

She sipped her coffee and focused her attention outside of the window and the people who were walking by looking as if their life were great and they didn't have a care in the world.

"Do you remember the day your father was killed?"

I nodded. "Like it was yesterday."

"Why did Stalyce say she killed him?"

"She didn't. But I know it was cause his bitch ass snitched on you."

She looked at me then back out the window quickly.

"Your father was sick. I don't hold his testimony against him." She said.

I became irritated by what she just said, "You fuckin' serious? Your best friend killed that nigga cause he had you locked up! He took you away from me and you don't hold that against him?" I shook my head in disgust at her.

She didn't like what I said and she leaned forward and smacked the table in front of me and stared me in my eyes. "I am still your mother and you will watch how the fuck you talk to me or I will make sure you join his ass!"

I sat back and closed my mouth. I nodded my head to her. "You got it."

She stayed in her position for a few seconds longer and then eased back into her seat.

"Would you like a cup of coffee?"

I shook my head. "I jus' wanna know whats goin' on and why you were with Tiffany."

"What you know 'bout her?"

"Enough."

"What's enough?"

"She a young chick I met, started fuckin' her and the sex was cool so I kept fuckin' wit' her 'til I was done wit' her."

She nodded. "What did I tell you about dealing wit' people?"

I didn't answer her.

"What rules did I give you to live by Devon?"

"I know the rules, Ma."

"But yet you broke every one of them and now instead of me being able to enjoy being free I have to come home and clean up your messes."

I was confused and I didn't have time for her riddles right now. "What are you talkin' 'bout Ma?"

She shook her head. "Everyone that comes into your life has an agenda. Whether that agenda is to genuinely love you and get to know you, or if it's to literally fuck you over; but they have an agenda. What you think that girl agenda was?"

"She know I am that nigga and she wanted to fuck wit' a real nigga." I said confidently.

"But why?"

"I don't know. That's what bitches do." I wasn't sure where this was going at all.

"I told you from get to let me know everyone you deal with didn't I?"

"Ma, you really wanted me to say hey Ma, I'm fuckin' this girl you know her?"

"Nigga I know you got a dick and I know you out here fuckin' but when I told you that it was because I needed to protect you the best way I could from there."

I sat back and folded my arms. "What you gettin' at man?"

"Tiffany was a job. Her job was to fuck you and fuck you over."

I laughed. If she was a job she was a damn good actress. "Ma, that girl ain't that smart."

She didn't blink.

"Ma, what you know? I need to know everything." I said sitting up realizing that things were about to go left real fast.

"Your father was a crackhead." She blurted out. My eyes widened. "He was sick."

I dropped my head and tried to remember any signs of my father showing that he was on drugs, but couldn't. When I didn't say anything she continued.

"A long time ago, right when we started making money, he started usin'. He did it only when he was kickin' it here and there, but then he got addicted. I'm not sure what it did to him on the inside cause on the outside he was able to keep it together."

The more she told me the story the less I wanted to be around her. I felt like she was full of secrets and been lying to me my whole life.

"I know that whatever those drugs was doin' to him was bringin' out the evil in him. He would be lettin' tricks suck his dick and all kind of shyt."

I frowned up my face.

"Then there was this one trick he served on the regular. He always would go over his house and they would get high together. This one day the dude didn't have the money so he offered him his son."

I didn't even want to hear any more of this sick ass story. "Ok, enough." I said putting my hand up as if to tell her to stop.

She ignored me. "He was forcing this kid to suck him off. I don't know why he chose that kid out of all the kids that were there because it was girls and boys there. Maybe he was so sick he enjoyed being with men, I don't know. But right when it was going on, the kid's older sister rushed in the room and hit her father on the head with a bottle and stabbed your dad in the leg."

"What the fuck?" my stomach was turning at this time. I wanted to throw up. My father was a faggot ass queer child molester and my mother stayed with him?

"I told you he was sick."

"What does this have to do with Tiff man?"

"She is the boy that was molested niece; his name is Deontae."

My eyes widened. "What?"

"I went to kill her and her family today."

"What? What the fuck is wrong wit' you? You jus' got out man?"

"It's either you or them." She didn't think what she was saying sounded crazy. She was convinced it all made sense.

"Well she still alive." I said wondering why if that's what she was really doing there.

"I can't kill her now."

"Why?"

"Your father also molested Bishop." She said changing the subject.

"Maaaaannnn, ok what the fuck else do I need to know because apparently my whole fuckin' life is a lie!"

"That's why Stalyce killed your father. Not because she was defending me. Because she was defending her son."

"She damn sure should've! I woulda killed that sick ass nigga too if I was her!"

"She blamed me for him molesting Bishop. She felt that I should have killed him when he was raping that uncle of Tiffany's."

I softened my attitude because my mother actually started to have some emotion in her voice.

"She put me in jail, Devon."

My eyes widened even more. I don't even think I was prepared for her to say that at all.

"What you mean *she* put you in jail?"

She sat up and got closer to me. "And for that I am going to kill her."

"Whoa, Ma. How you know she did this?" I had to be sure.

"I can read Devon. I read who said what against me and the things they knew only she knew. I knew she was going to kill your father, she told me. I couldn't do it. I loved him. He was my husband and as fucked up as it sounds he never touched you."

"Damn right that nigga never fuckin' touched me." I said reinsuring her. "That's probably why Bishop confused and fuckin' niggas."

"Probably." She agreed.

"Does she know you know?"

She shook her head.

"I can't lie, the shyt sound crazy cause she always treated me like her own, but you are my mother and whatever you wanna do I'm down for."

She smiled. "I want you to go back to Miami and live."

"Nah, I'm not doin' that until I handle the loose ends here, starting with Tiffany." I said.

She shook her head. "Don't touch that girl."

"You jus' told me that I was a job fo' the bitch now I can't touch her?"

She shook her head. "I've said enough for the day. Jus' let me handle her."

I stared at her knowing it was more that she had to tell me and I honestly couldn't imagine what else there was to tell, but anything was possible now.

"Ok. I'll play by your rules. For now."

"Thank you."

"I got somethin' to do tho', Ma, so Imma get up outta here and I'll see you later?" I said standing up.

She nodded. "Coming home feels like a whole new world. Nothin' looks the same." She continued to stare out the window.

"Tell me 'bout it. I've only been gone almost a year and it's completely different." I said as my eyes followed to what she was staring at.

I focused to make sure my eyes wasn't playin' tricks on me. Right there was Tiffany and Keyona hugging and kissing leaned up against the same Altima I saw her leave in.

"Well, shut the fuck up. I'll be damned."

I wasn't sure if I was shocked at the fact they were kissing or the fact my mother came here just to keep an eye on her. I couldn't deny watching two of my hoes kiss had me turned on slightly.

One thing that was for sure was every move my

mother made definitely had a motive and a lot of thought behind it. Even though she told me not to follow her she was anyway and the whole time we were talking she was watching her. I couldn't do anything but respect it.

"Startin' to get it now?"

I nodded.

"I don't know what her uncle looks like now that he is grown. Don't touch her Devon. Let me handle it. She will take me to him soon. If I'm right about her and the reason she is in your life, I'm sure she will be goin' to see him soon."

I folded my arms and nodded my head. I knew I was smart and that's how I survived the streets, but my mother was ahead of it all. I was willing to learn a few things from her.

Tiffany

"You definitely got some explainin' to do!" I shouted at my uncle as I followed him around his house.

"I don't have to explain shyt." He snapped never giving me any attention.

"Yes the fuck you do!" I wasn't backing down from him today.

He stopped and turned to me and got closer to me so that we were face to face. He was taller than me so I made sure my stance was strong just in case he tried to hit me or grab me and made sure I showed him no fear as I looked up into his eyes.

He smirked at me. "Get the fuck out Tiff."

"I'm not goin' no fuckin' where! Why is she callin' you Baby? Why were you at her house?"

"Why is she callin' you her cousin? Why were you at her house?" he asked still smirking at me.

"You asked me to find Black so that's what I was doin'!" I lied.

"Who do you think you talkin' to Tiff? The bitch called you her cousin, you doin' more than that wit' her."

"How long, Unk?"

"How long what?"

"How long you been over there wit' her? What

you know?" I asked hoping he would tell me more.

We had a staring match for about five minutes and it was completely silent. I wasn't going to back down this time. I needed to know what he knew so I could plan my next move.

"Sit down Tiff."

I paused then sat on his white Italian leather sofa. The more I seen in his house the desperate I was to have a home just like his and I would stop at nothing to get it and I wouldn't let anyone, including him, get in the way of that.

"I met her a few months back at a club and didn't know that was her until recently."

I knew he was lying. I didn't let him know I knew he was lying because I wanted to see how far he would go with it. Everybody knew who Juicy was. Everybody knew she was the coldest booster in Cleveland and could get you anything you wanted and everyone knew that she was Black's baby mama.

"Then when I realized who she was I decided to take advantage of it."

"Why do you want Black so bad?"

He got quiet.

I felt like I had to pick until he snapped and told me. "His mother came to see me the other day."

His eyes widened. "What?"

"Black never was hiding when he was in Cleveland. Ever. It was so many times you could have got him, but didn't. You knew when he was around me and when he left me. I'm beginning to think you fraud."

I knew that hit a soft spot with him because he stood up and jumped at me. "Bitch the only fraud here is you!"

I smirked. Now he was the one out of control, but I needed to know why he wanted him so bad. He could have robbed Black a thousand times when I thought about it.

It's like he had this sick obsession with him. He knew everything about him; who his crew was, where he hung out, now he was fuckin' Juicy? I felt like his hatred was strong because he wanted to be him.

"Why did his mother come see you? When did she get out?" he asked in a calmer tone.

I shrugged. "She got word that she had a grandbaby and came to see her."

"How?"

I shrugged again. "It's Cleveland. People talk."

"So Black was with her?"

"I said *his* mother came. Not him." I said sarcastically.

"If she out then he not far behind."

"Maybe."

"Did you ask her?"

I shook my head.

"Why?"

"She wouldn't tell me anyway. The bitch is weird as fuck."

"Weird? What you mean she weird?"

"I don't know. I couldn't put a finger on it. Her eyes look empty and she doesn't smile at all. Even when she held Teonna, she just stared."

"She ain't weird. She up to somethin'."

"Like what? Maybe she lookin' for Black too then."

He shook his head. "Nah, she knows where he at. What she look like?"

"I don't know. Brown skin, toned up. About my height. She don't look old at all. She got like this sexy Angela Basset thing goin' for her."

"So she looks the same as she always did."

I shrugged. "I don't know, but my mother knew who she was the minute she came in the house."

He nodded. "I know she did. Was she scared?"

I was confused. "Why would she be scared of her?"

"Watch her. When is she coming back over?"

"I don't know. She didn't say. What you got planned for Juicy?"

"Nothin'."

"You gon' kill her?" I asked praying inside he said no.

He shook his head. "I don't need her now that his mother back. I can find him through her."

"Man, what the fuck this nigga do to you? I need to know."

"Let me know when she comes back over. I need to talk to your mother."

"Bet." I said knowing I wasn't going to tell him anything, but I needed to go see Juicy because I didn't trust him when it comes to her.

I stood up. "I gotta go."

He nodded.

"We will talk soon."

He nodded again. I turned and walked out he house as I heard him board his door behind me. I wasn't sure what was going on or what Black's mama was up to, but I wanted to be prepared for whatever they brought my way. As soon as I hopped in my car I called Juicy.

To my surprise she answered on the first ring. "I need to holla at you."

"Me too. Stop by." She said and hung up on me.

I looked at the phone and frowned my face. Her tone was different and I was almost willing to bet she figured out something about my uncle.

I know the saying is blood is thicker than water, but when it came to him I didn't feel like it was and I really felt like Juicy would be loyal to me before he would; so my thought was to warn her. My only problem would be if she believed me or not or thought I was going to set her up too.

Juicy

"Here I come." I said as I walked down to the side door to let Tiffany in.

She called and said she needed to talk to me and I was glad because I had to see how she really knew Tae. He tried to have me thinking it was nothing, but I was no fool and if they were setting me up or on some bull shyt I was going to make sure I got both of them before they got me. I knew I couldn't trust her ass and I should have went with my first mind when it came to her.

I tied my hair up as I stepped down the last step and opened the door. My heart stopped for a moment and I thought I was seeing things. I opened the door without looking assuming it was Tiffany, but it was Black.

My first thought was to run back for my gun because if he were standing at my door meant that he figured out we set him up and framed him for what we did and I have known him long enough to know that when Black came for you he was coming for blood.

"Oh my God!" I said panicking.

He gave me a side look and I took off running up the stairs back to my bedroom. He didn't wait to see what I was running for or ask any questions because just like I knew him he knew me and he knew I was running for my gun.

I skid across the kitchen and hit my right shoulder on the doorway leading to the hallway toward my bedroom. I screamed when I turned and saw him quick on my heels.

I panicked and picked up the pace and ran into my room and dived toward my bed. To my surprise when I dived he did too and landed directly on me.

I screamed. "Get off me!"

I did my best to wiggle and kick him off of me, but he was strong. Black was much stronger and heavier than I remembered and I couldn't move him at all.

"Please! Get off of me!" I kept screaming and kicking.

He saw me reaching my right arm toward my night stand and he grabbed my arms and pulled them downward and crossed them as his grip tightened on me.

"Black! Please! Your hurtin' me!"

"Why the fuck you runnin'?" he asked.

"Why the fuck you here!" I continued to move around trying to release his grip, but the more I squirmed the harder his grip got.

"I'm not here to hurt you! I just wanted to see DJ!" he yelled.

I stopped moving and stared him in the eyes. My breathing was heavy and so was his. He relaxed on top of me and started to loosen the grip he had.

"If you reach for that gun I'm knockin' you the fuck out."

I knew he meant what he was saying and I just relaxed my body and stopped moving. I felt my face was wet and didn't realize I was crying.

He was still kneeled sitting on top of me and I couldn't help but to notice he was bigger than he used to be. He had on a white wife beater, something he never wore out of the house before, and some grey jogging pants with some Black Gamma Air Jordan's on and he smelled so good. He was sweaty from our tussle.

He noticed I was crying and took his left hand and wiped my tears from my face. I closed my eyes because even though we left things on a bad note I still had love for him. We were together for a long time and at the time we split things were bad between us.

"I never got a chance to say I was sorry." I said opening my eyes.

He pulled his hand back and rested them on his knees. He didn't say anything he just dropped his head.

"I really am Devon. I never wanted to hurt you. Jus' at the time I was so mad at you and shyt was jus' fucked up between us and when it got bad it just got worse from there."

He got off of me and sat on the floor next to me and bent his legs and laid his arms on top as his right hand held his left.

"Where is DJ?"

"The bus should be dropping him off soon." I could tell he didn't care about my apology by the way he changed the subject.

"You lookin' good I said as I sat up and adjusted my tank and shorts.

The compliment must have got to him because he cracked a half smile.

"Yeah you are too." He said looking down between his legs.

I got closer to him and touched his cheek softly. "I really never meant to hurt you." I said to make sure he believed me this time.

I was relieved to know that he didn't know about how we framed him for the robbery. I wouldn't be able to take it if he knew the truth. I felt I did enough to hurt him already.

He let me touch him for a few seconds then he moved away. I put my hand on my leg and waited until he was at ease again.

"Why though?"

"I don't know. I was young and dumb at the time."

"I was young too, but I loved you."

I knew he did. He loved me from day one. I loved him later in our relationship, but my heart was always with Bishop.

"You did some fucked up shyt too tho' Black." I reminded him.

"Fucked up to where I deserved that tho', Juicy?" he looked me in my face. "Nah, no man deserves that kinda karma."

"You right."

"Where he at tho'?" he asked trying to get off our past.

"Therapy."

His eyes widened. "For what?"

I dropped my head. "He's in a wheel chair and has to learn to walk again."

He gripped his hands and dropped his head. "This is my fault."

I dropped my head because it was really my fault. I should have been home with my son instead of sleeping with Bishop when he got shot.

Black stood up and went over to my dresser. I had a picture of Tae taped to the left corner.

"New man?" he asked as he got a closer look at the picture.

I stood up and pulled my shorts back down my thighs and walked to where he was. "Somethin' like that."

He smirked with a slight laugh. "Does DJ like him?"

I was embarrassed to answer him. "They haven't met."

He nodded. "Probably for the best."

I paused for a minute. That wasn't what I expected him to say. "Why is that?"

"Every nigga you fuck don't need to meet him." He said as he leaned against the dresser and crossed his arms.

I was surprised to see that he still cared. He was gone for so long without any signs of where he could be I assumed he was done with all of us completely. I wanted to reach out to Peaches a few times to see how he was, but I was too embarrassed to talk to her after what I did.

"Does he ask about me?"

I lied immediately. "All the time."

I couldn't hurt him by telling him the truth that DJ didn't ever ask about him and that he probably didn't even remember him. He smiled and looked down at the floor.

"I wanted to call him every day I was gone."

I walked closer to him because I wanted to hug him. I don't know why, it was just in me to want to touch him like I used to do. Tae briefly popped in my head, but I focused back to Black quickly.

He stared at me as I moved closer to him and didn't say anything. I felt like he wanted me to by the way he was looking at me. As reached in slowly and moved his hands apart I could feel my heart beat faster.

I took both of his hands and wrapped them around me and hugged him around his neck. Our eyes never lost contact and he leaned in and kissed me. I closed my eyes and began to kiss him back. I got lost in the moment when the doorbell rang and broke me out of our trance. I didn't want to stop kissing him. It felt normal and familiar.

He pulled back and let me go. "I'm married."

My eyes widened. "What?"

"I'm married." He repeated as he stepped back away from me.

"No, I heard what the fuck you said, but what the fuck you mean you *married,* Black?" I snapped as if we were still together.

He dropped his head. "Answer the door."

I stared at him for a minute and I wanted to cry. I

was with him for years and marriage was never an option for us. If I recalled he said he never wanted to get married or even believed in marriage.

"Who the fuck is she?" I needed to know.

"You don't know her."

"Where she from?"

"You don't know her." He repeated.

"So you jus' up and get married out of no fuckin' where to some random bitch and I was the one who had put up wit' all your shyt for years!" I yelled still in disbelief.

"She not a random bitch. I've known her a few years. And chill wit' the bull shyt. You didn't loyally put up wit' shyt. You was fuckin' Bishop the whole time and God knows who else." He reminded me.

My heart felt like it was broken in a million pieces when he said that. I know I did some fucked up shyt to him, but I think this was the worse. I had to know who she was and why she was special that he married her and never even considered me even before he found out about DJ not being his.

"Why her?"

"Don't do this."

"I need to know. Why her?" I begged for an answer.

"Because I love her. I'm in love with her." He said as

he looked me in my eyes.

I folded my arms and looked him up and down. "Hmmm. Well not too much because you jus' forgot 'bout the bitch a few minutes ago when you had your tongue down my throat!"

He waved his hand at me. "Man watch out."

I turned and walked out the room to go answer the door when I remembered Tiffany was supposed to stop by and that's who was ringing the doorbell. I didn't want her and Black to see each other because there was no way I could talk my way out of that with him.

I walked to the side door quickly hoping that he wouldn't follow me. There was Tiffany standing there looking around as if she was irritated. I cracked the door and started to whisper to her.

"I need you to leave and I'll call you later and explain."

She squinted her eyes at me. "What's wrong?"

"Black is here and I need you to go!" I whispered.

Her face lit up. "Black? I need to talk to him!" she tried to open the door and I pushed her back immediately.

"Bitch you gon' get us caught! I'll make sure he get at you, jus' go!"

She stopped for a second. "Make sure he do and I

really gotta talk to you."

I nodded. "Okay, now leave before he see you!" I closed the door in her face and prayed he didn't hear anything I was saying to her.

I walked back to my bedroom and he wasn't there. I should have known he would be listening. I walked around the hallway to the living room and he was standing there looking out of the picture window with his arms crossed. I knew he had seen Tiffany then.

"So you two friends now?"

I didn't answer.

"See I had a feeling that it was her that robbed Bishop and them, had me set up and then I thought nah it wasn't her because she not that smart. And then I wondered who could she have done that with and never in a million years would I have guessed you." He laughed as he said our entire plan out loud.

I didn't say anything. My heart started to beat and I wondered what he was going to do to me after he said that.

"That was smart. Your plan?" he asked as he turned face to face with me.

I shook my head.

"Hers?" he asked with a look of amazement as he used his thumb to point behind him.

I nodded.

He smiled again and nodded his head as he folded his arms again.

"I'm impressed."

"What are you goin' to do?" I was afraid to ask.

"On the strength of DJ, nothin' to you. But her-" I immediately cut him off. "And on the strength of Teonna, please don't do nothin' to her."

He looked confused. "Who?"

I knew it wasn't my place to tell him about him having a daughter, but I know Black and he would have killed Tiffany on GP just because she set him up. I knew he didn't care about the money at all, it was always the principle with him.

"Your daughter."

"What? What the fuck you talkin' 'bout."

"Tiffany has a baby by you. She been tryin' to find you for months to tell you." I was hoping this took his attention from what we did to him.

"What?" he asked again. "Nah. How you know its my baby?"

"She look jus' like you."

"Fuck outta here, that's the same shyt you said about DJ and you see how that ended!" he snapped.

"I'm not lying. You have a daughter."

He stepped back and sat on the sofa in front of me.

"How am I goin' to tell my wife this shyt?" he said to himself as he dropped his head.

I instantly became angry at him. I wondered if he ever cared that much about my feelings when he was out doing the shyt he was doing behind my back.

I folded my arms and smirked. I didn't know her, but I was glad the bitch was getting the same kind of pains I had to deal with when I was with him. I didn't feel sorry for her either. I desperately wanted to find out who she was though. He said he knew her a few years so I'm sure I had to have heard of her at least once.

We were quiet for about ten minutes and I could tell he was nervous about what just told him.

"You really are in love with her, huh?"

He looked up at me and made a face as if he hated me. "How do you know this kid doesn't belong to Juvey?"

I forgot she even slept with Juvey because when you look at Teonna she was the spit and image of Black. She looked more like Black than she did Tiffany.

Before I could answer him DJ's bus horn interrupted. "I gotta grab DJ off the bus."

I turned to walk away and he stood up and followed me. By the time I got to the end of the driveway the driver had already taken him off the bus and was pushing his chair toward me. I glanced behind me and Black was right next to me. I don't know why, but I was nervous about them seeing each other right now.

DJ's face lit up. He stood up out of his chair slowly and I paused. He did remember Black. The driver got on the bus and pulled off. Black walked over to DJ kneeled down in front of him.

"Hey DJ."

He smiled.

DJ took his hands and grabbed onto both of Black's shoulders and used them to hold himself up. He was still learning to walk again in therapy so what he was doing right now I could tell was hard for him, but he was doing it.

"Do you remember me?"

DJ nodded.

"Who am I?"

"You're my dad." He said as he wrapped his arms around his neck and hugged him tight.

I stepped back and covered my mouth and started to cry. I really fucked up big.

Black

Seeing DJ for the first time in months hurt more than I thought it would. I couldn't believe he was in a wheel chair and I had just up and disappeared on him. The pain I was feeling seeing that hurt almost as bad as when I found out he wasn't mine.

I couldn't stop holding him though. It felt good to see my son. In my heart he was still my son and apparently in his I was still his dad. I wondered how close he had gotten to Bishop in the last few months.

"Juicy, gimme a minute wit' him." I said never looking at her.

She had the nerve to be crying as if she was so shocked when he said I was his dad. I was still trying to process what she told me about Tiffany. I would deal with that when I left here because it was no way in hell she had a baby by me.

I pushed DJ chair to the back yard to talk to him so that I wouldn't be seen if anyone was to ride up the street.

"I knew you was coming back." DJ said as I sat on a chair so that we could be face to face.

"Oh yeah?"

He nodded. "Bishop said not to talk about you to

my mommy."

I was confused. "Why is that?"

He shrugged. "He said it makes her cry."

"Who is Bishop to you?" I asked to see what story they gave him.

"He my real dad."

I nodded. Hearing him say that hurt me deep. "Yeah."

"But he told me that you my first dad and if something happen to him that you coming to get me."

I nodded again. "Bishop said that?"

He nodded. "Can I go with you when you leave?"

I shook my head. "I wish you could."

He dropped his head. "But I will come back and see you.

"Okay."

I gave him a hug and kissed his forehead then took him in the house. I had to go find out about Tiffany and then it dawned on me; that's why my mother didn't go through with killin' her, she saw my daughter.

What I don't get is if she saw her and knew she was my daughter why wouldn't she have told me and why did she lie and tell me I was sterile and couldn't have any kids.

I got in my car to head back to the hotel to check

on Aariona. As I dialed her number I noticed a car following me. At first it seemed as if the car was just making the same turns as me, but as I slowed down so I could pay attention I noticed it was Tiffany.

I had switched rentals yesterday and knew that after she saw me I had to switch again. Since she was following me I decided to make her follow me some where I could talk to her without being recognized. I led her Tinker Creek in Valley View where I knew there weren't going to be anyone we knew there.

She didn't know I knew she was following me and I made sure she couldn't tell I was watching her.

I continued to watch my rear view as she slowed up trying not to be seen. I was amused by her. I always thought she was the dingy naïve type, but she fooled me.

"Hello!" Aariona shouted.

I was so distracted by watching Tiffany in my mirrors that I forgot I called her.

"Sorry baby, how you feelin'?

"I'm bored."

"Go to the workout room and walk on the treadmill." I suggested still only giving her minimum attention.

"No! Let's just go home. We can forget this happened. I don't want to be here and I don't want to have my baby here or alone!"

She gained my full attention when she said that. "Forget this happened? Do you know who I am?"

"Who you are? Are you serious Devon?"

"You think that I'm gon' let a nigga get away wit' that shyt, Aariona?" I snapped.

"Is this about your ego or me? Because if it's about your ego I am on the next flight back home!" she yelled.

"Aariona we'll talk." I said as I hung up on her and pulled into a parking space.

I didn't have time for her tantrums right now. We were going through those talks too often and I was sick of it. I sat in my car and looked in the mirror as I watch Tiffany dumb ass park in the row behind me, but across the way so she could watch me.

I slipped my gun under my seat and hopped out the car. She slid down slightly like she was trying not to be seen. I pretended to walk toward where the picnic tables were so that I didn't alarm her and acted as if I didn't see her. Once I got near her car I grabbed the driver door and yanked it open so fast and she gasped as if she seen a ghost.

I didn't have the same bond or love with Tiffany I once had with Juicy so I didn't feel any remorse at all right now. I was so pissed that she set me up and was still acting as if she ran things by following me right now.

I grabbed her by her hair and pulled her out the car as hard as I could. She hit the ground and I drug her across the park. The park was empty right now; I assume the people that had parked their cars there were walking the trail or in the creek and I was glad because I didn't need any interruptions right now.

"Ah! Stop!" she screamed as she tried her hardest to loosen my grip. "Black! Stop!"

I ignored her screams and continued to drag her by her hair. "Stupid bitch! You set me up!"

I kept in mind that she may possibly be the mother of my child so I wasn't going to hurt her too bad, but she was going to feel it right now.

I let her hair go and she stood up as fast as she could. She was breathing heavy, but she wasn't crying. She paused to catch her breath as she stared me in my eyes.

I waited to see what she was going to say next, but instead she charged at me. I stepped back and took my right hand and mugged her in her face as hard as I could. She fell back onto the ground.

"Bitch!" she screamed when she hit the ground.

I wanted to punch her in her mouth but instead I stood over her and just continued to mug her as hard as I could.

"What the fuck you followin' me fo'? I asked in between mugging her.

Her head would jerk back and forth and she would try to block my hand, but I was stronger than her.

"Don't fuckin' touch me!"

I could tell she wanted to cry right now because her voice began to crack. I stopped mugging her so that she could talk. I looked down at her clothes. She had on an all -white jogging suite that was covered in dirt from me dragging her across the park. I laughed.

"I jus' wanted to tell you 'bout your fuckin' daughter!"

"Oh yeah? When was you gon' fuckin' tell me how you set me up?" I asked as I mugged her again.

Her head jerked back and she didn't say a word. She looked nervous as if she was wondering how I found out.

"Yeah, bitch I know 'bout it!" I mugged her again.

Anyone else I would have killed off top, but because she *might* have my kid I just roughed her up.

"You wasn't supposed to come back."

I shook my head. "Who does the kid really belong to?" I asked switching the subject.

"You."

I shook my head. "Impossible."

"Take a fuckin' test! I don't care! And when you do, take her with you!" she yelled.

I frowned my face. "Bitch what the fuck wrong wit' you?"

"That's why I been lookin' for you. So I can give you your child." She said quietly.

I stood straight up realizing she was serious. "I have a daughter?"

She nodded.

"I can't take her."

"Why not?" she said as she stood up and stepped out my arms reach.

"I'm married."

Her face dropped. "What?

"I have a kid with my wife."

"What the fuck you say?" she yelled as she began throwing punches.

She continued to swing as hard as she could with both hands, but not one landed. I continued to duck and dodge them making her tire herself out. I started to laugh as she tried her hardest to hit me; me laughing at her was pissing her off even more and she finally landed a punch across my jaw.

Out of reflex I smacked her across her cheek and she

fell back to the ground. I didn't mean to hit her as hard as I did, but I wasn't going to apologize for it either.

This must have been the icing on the cake because she started to cry. A part of me wanted to kneel down and help her up, but I didn't. I stood over her emotionless and I let it show on my face that I didn't care she was hurt.

"I give up!" she cried.

"Good."

"I jus' want her to know you." She said as she continued to cry.

I didn't say anything. I really didn't want to see the baby at all. I was content with just having a son with my wife, but I know that wasn't reality and I would be less of a man if I didn't at least make sure if she belonged to me.

"What about Juvey? How you know that not his baby?"

She wiped her face and stood up. "Because dumb ass I was already pregnant when me and him started fuckin'!"

I didn't care about Juvey smashin' her while I was, but this hoe had to be crazy to think that she was goin' to brag about it so I back handed her in her mouth.

Her bottom lip started bleeding and she grabbed her mouth and wiped the blood as she looked at it on her fingers then back at me. It was all over her face that she wanted to hit me back, but I think she realized this was a fight she was going to lose.

"Make you feel like a man hittin' me huh?" she said sarcastically.

"Bitch, the only reason I ain't kill you for that bull shyt set up is 'cause you *might* be the mother of my child!"

She shook her head. "You're pathetic."

"Where's the money at?"

She stepped back. "It's gone."

She was lying. I laughed at her and shook my head. "Who helped you?"

"What makes you think Imma tell you anything after you just did all this to me?"

She did change from the Tiffany I remember. I wondered if that whole time the innocent young girl thing was just an act and my mother was right.

It was quiet for a moment and I came to the conclusion she wasn't going to tell me anything so I let it be.

"When can I see the baby?"

She shrugged. "When do you want to take the test?"

"Is that the only way I can see her?"

She nodded.

I smirked. "I'll let you know."

She started to back up and go to her car, but never turning her back on me. I could tell she was afraid of me now and was concerned about what I would do to her. I folded my arm and watched her walk to her car.

She got in her car and pulled out her parking spot and turned her car around and came on the opposite side I was on and hit the brakes. We locked eyes for a minute and she didn't blink.

Before I could say anything she pulled out a gun and shot twice in my direction. *Pop! Pop!* I dove behind a car that was near me. She caught me off guard and my heart was beating fast.

"Put your hands on me again Bitch and next time I won't miss!" she yelled out and quickly peeled off.

I stayed on the ground by the car realizing that she missed on purpose and that was just her way of scaring me. I started laughing after I sat there alone for a few minutes. That bitch was crazy.

Tiffany

I was crying as I sped as fast as I could from Tinker Creek after I shot at Black. I wasn't going to kill him, but I had to let him know I wasn't the same dumb ass girl he used to be with.

I looked in my mirrors to see if he was following me, but he wasn't so I slowed down and started to do the speed limit. I glanced down at my all white Gucci jogging suit.

I couldn't believe he had yanked me out the car the way he did. My head was throbbing from where he was pulling my hair and dragging me across the grass. I realized he knew I was following him the entire time and he led me there so he could do that to me.

I know I deserved it and probably more because I almost had him killed, but I wasn't going to just let him do me any kind of way. I called Juicy so that I could go warn her about my uncle and make sure she still trusted me.

"Hey." She answered.

I tried to sound normal. "I really need to talk to you."

"What's wrong? Why you sound like that?" she asked.

"Me and Black jus' fought."

"What? Where are you?" she sounded concerned.

"Can I come back now?"

"Yeah come on."

I pulled into her driveway this time. It really didn't matter anymore about parking a few houses down. Now everyone knew that we had some kind of connection. Before I could knock on the door she opened it.

"Oh my God, what happened?" she asked looking at how dirty my clothes were and my hair was all over the place. She checked behind me before she closed the door and I went and sat at her kitchen table.

"I waited for him to leave your house and I started to follow him." I began.

I was shaking my right leg as I sat there because I was still shook up and nervous. I knew Black wasn't the type to beat women, but I also knew he didn't play no games and if you deserved an ass whoopin', man or woman, he wouldn't hesitate to give it to you.

She shook her head at me as she sat down across from me. "I told you I would make sure he talked to you. That nigga ain't dumb. He saw you here and figured out our whole plan!"

I squinted my eyes at her. "Why would you

confirm it tho'?"

"Huh?"

"When he figured out why didn't you jus' lie and say I was here askin' for you to find him so he could meet his daughter?"

She went blank. "I didn't think about that."

I nodded at I pierced my lips together. "Obviously."

"Well the only reason you got your ass beat and not killed was cause I told him about your daughter!" she tried to clean it up.

"Look, Juicy, that's not what I'm here for."

She sat back in her chair and crossed her arms. I could tell she was on the defense before I even started to explain why I wanted to talk to her.

"How long have you been dealin' wit' Tae?"

"A few months. How you know him?" she gave me her full attention and eye contact when I mentioned him.

"Did you know we knew each other already?"

She nodded. "The way you looked at him I could tell you did, but what I was wondering is if it was jus' a coincidence that you both knew me."

"No coincidence." I admitted.

She shook her head and crossed her arms again.

"You sneaky-"

I cut her off and put my hand up to signaling to stop. "I'm not against you."

She looked away.

"Juicy, I know we never said it to each other, but I fucks wit' you. I know how we met was on some bull shyt, but you grew on me."

She turned her attention back to me.

"And what I'm about to tell you, I'm only sayin' it cause I feel like you would do the same."

"I'm listenin'."

I took a deep breath and hoped that this all wouldn't come back to bite me in the ass. "Tae is my uncle."

She squinted her eyes at me but didn't interrupt so I continued.

"His original plan was to have me date Black, find out where he stay at then he come rob him."

"You fuckin' serious?"

I nodded.

"But Black was so secretive I never knew where he stayed or laid his head at. I always assumed it was in the Valley wit' you."

"So why is he wit' me now then?"

I shrugged. "That I don't know. It's like he has

some sick obsession wit' Black. I assume he hate him 'cause he wanna be him so he fuckin' wit' you 'cause he know Black ain't in Cleveland no more."

She got quiet and stared off in the other direction.

"How am I supposed to believe you? How do I know you aint jus' tryin' to cover up the fact I know about you and him now?"

"Why would I tell on my uncle if I was lyin'?"

"Exactly. Why would you?"

I sucked my teeth. "That nigga don't give a fuck 'bout me Juicy! You probably care more 'bout me than he do!"

She didn't respond she just stared at me; she was trying to read me so I let her.

"Look, I care and I think he up to somthin' wit' you and I jus' want you aware. You can't trust him. Period."

"But I can trust you, huh?" she asked in a sarcastic tone.

"For the most part, yeah." I admitted.

"Fair enough."

"So now what?" I asked.

She shrugged. "I don't know. It's fucked up you can't trust *nobody*."

I nodded. I really didn't know what else to say to

her.

"So we still game about the Prive?"

I nodded. "What 'bout Bishop?"

She shrugged. "Now that Black is back I don't know which way to go."

I was confused. "What he got to do wit' it?"

"Cause he might take the hit for that too. It's gone look like he came back after robbin' him to kill him."

I hadn't thought about that. I didn't want him to go down for murder because of Teonna. I sat back and stared away trying to think of something. I had nothing.

"Let's jus' go through with the Prive shyt."

"Okay. What you gon' do 'bout Tae?" I was curious.

She shrugged. "I don't know."

I shook my head. "He made you love him didn't he?"

She nodded.

"Well don't! Remember it was all fake! Anything he ever said to you wasn't real."

She stared at me and I saw a tear escape her right eye and a left one followed. She didn't even bother to wipe her face. I knew she was hurt, but I felt like she needed to know the truth.

"Man, don't cry."

"I jus' don't understand why every nigga the same."

I had no response for her. Part of me was hoping she took the info and used it to have my uncle taken out, but she was in love and I could tell that it would take for him to hurt her himself before she made a move. She probably took what I told her as hatin' and really believed it was real between them.

I couldn't worry about that right now. I just hoped she didn't tell him what I told her because he would definitely come for me then.

I waited to see if she was going to say anything else and when she didn't I stood up to leave.

"Thursday?" I asked.

She nodded.

"Aight, don't get choked up again, makin' us have to postpone this shyt again." I said joking to lighten the mood.

She stood up and gave a half a laugh. "Tuh, you one to talk. Look like Black drug your ass all around the street."

I stopped smiling. "He did, Bitch. Literally."

She looked at me and burst out laughing. I paused and couldn't help but to laugh with her.

"I can picture his ass draggin' you too!" she

continued to laugh.

"Shut up! It aint funny!" I said as I laughed a little more with her.

As I thought about it I couldn't help but to laugh at it too. I wondered what he was thinkin' when I shot at him too.

"I bet his ass won't touch me again tho'; I shot my gun at his punk ass when I hopped in the car."

She stopped laughing. "You serious?"

I nodded.

"Well, did you shoot him? I mean what happened?" she sounded scared when she asked me.

It amazed me to see Juicy in her vulnerable moments because she always had this tough heartless gangsta chick thing goin' on in public; but behind closed doors she was soft as fuck.

I shook my head. "Nothin'. I got in the car, shot at him, well near him, he ducked and I sped off."

"So you didn't shoot him?"

I shook my head. "Nah. I don't think so. I jus' wanted to scare him."

She put her right hand on her forehead like she was shocked. You don't *scare* Black; either you kill him or don't pull your gun out."

I frowned. "What you sayin'?"

"Watch your back. He don't let shyt slide like that." She said as she folded her arms.

I looked at her and didn't say anything. For some reason I wasn't afraid of him coming after me.

"Aight. I'm gone."

"Yup." She said as she followed me to lock her side door.

I knew the next few days were going to be wild and I was really hoping to find out who this woman he so called married. When he told me that I immediately changed my mind about letting my daughter go live with him so I told him he had to take a test before he saw her. He wasn't about to have my daughter calling some bitch *Mommy*.

Juicy

"Oooh....damn baby..." I moaned as Tae explored my body as if it were his first time with the tip of his tongue.

I couldn't stop him right now even though my mind was screaming *get this nigga the fuck off of you Juicy; just reach under your pillow and put a bullet in his* head *before he kills you;* but my body was saying something totally different.

My body was screaming louder than my mind right now. It was like the devil and the angel on your shoulder in both ears telling you which way to go and right now my body was winning.

When I was with Tae I felt like my soul connected with his. A small voice that was Tiffany's voice to be exact echoed in my head *"Remember it was all fake!"*

It didn't feel fake right now. The way he kissed all over me slowly. Paying extra attention to my spots; first my lips as he made his way to the left side of my neck while his left hand slowly caressed my breast and his right hand had a tight, but enticing grip on my hair.

He continued to grind his naked body against mine and even though the central air was on our bodies were hot and beginning to sweat the more he kissed me and pressed against me.

He never went inside me; he just continued to make my body beg for him until my kitty started to leak against his thigh letting him know she was more than ready to feel him. He stopped kissing on me and looked me in my eyes as he rubbed my hair to the back.

"No matter what happens between us, know that I love you and how I feel is real."

I didn't say anything. It was like he was reading my mind. I stared him in his eyes and no matter how long I stared I couldn't find the insincerity in his eyes. I felt like he meant everything he was saying and doing right now because the kind of chemistry we have right now can't be faked.

When I began to speak he slid his tongue in my mouth and began to massage my clit slowly with his left thumb. I let out a small moan in between our kisses.

I couldn't think about anything Tiffany told me right now. Tae owned my mind, body and soul. I was his and only his right now. The moon light shined through my blinds as the music played softly and I felt him slowly slide in side me and I let my head rest back on the pillow as I moaned his name softly. The mood was perfect.

"Ahhh Taeeee…"

I moaned as I pulled him closer. He was already close as he could be; it was like I wanted us to become one as long as we could, I wanted our passion to connect and stay that way for as long as it could.

Nothing mattered, but us right now. Not Black, not Tiffany, Bishop or any of the bull shyt I was dealing with outside of this moment.

"Ooohh Michaela…" he moaned as he moved inside me slowly.

I paused. *Michaela*? He has never called me by my real name. The trance he had me in was broken. He had me under some kind of spell for a minute until he said that. It made me come off the high he took me on mentally and back to reality.

Something inside me said that Tiffany was telling the truth; it was all fake. Some may call that something that speaks to you your conscious; intuition; or even the voice of God. Whoever it was talking to me right now I was listening finally.

Even though he could fake how he felt, I couldn't. I felt all the intensity between us suppress. The music was still going and the old school mix I had playing in the background that once put me in the mood was beginning to irritate me almost instantly.

Every song that was on the mix was a song that

reminded me of him and it began to sound like a tune of lies. *R. Kelly's The Greatest Sex* was next in line and I could feel my heart dropping as I realized he played me. I was sleeping with the enemy; a real enemy.

The enemy who I couldn't tell if he was *just* after Black or was he after me as well. When I realized how much in danger I really was I felt myself begin to dry up. Tae was still moving in and out of me slowly when he finally realized I wasn't into it as I was at first.

He stopped and pulled back to look at me. The light wasn't on so he could only see what the light of the moon revealed to him; which was my eyes although I could see his face very well because the way the light fell was in my favor.

I knew my eyes told on me every time; it was something I could never control so when our eyes locked he knew something was wrong.

"What's wrong?" he hesitantly asked.

I said nothing I just stared as all kind of thoughts ran through my mind. Technically he was still in control. He was on top of me and if I revealed what I knew about him he would definitely be able to get to my gun before I could.

I started to beat myself up mentally. How could I have been so stupid? From the day we met began to make sense to me. How he didn't talk to any female at the club and made sure I knew he wanted me and *only* me.

I was his mark; his target. He knew what he was coming there for and it was me. He had done to me what Tiffany and I were planning to do to some poor sucka from EC. I was from the Valley; the streets made me and I somehow fell for *this*?

I jumped out of my feelings quickly as I remembered who I was and where I came from. Then I remembered I wasn't home alone and my son was in the next room sleeping so I had to be smart right now.

"Let's get married." I threw that out there.
It was the first thing I could think of to throw him off. Somewhere in the back of mind I was still upset about Black being married so I think that is why it came out before I could think of anything else and if there was anything I knew that would throw a nigga off and make him fall back was to say your pregnant or you want to get married. We didn't have sex enough to throw out the pregnancy card so I played the first one I could. I felt him go limp while he was inside me. *Good* I thought.

"What?" he asked with a low cracked voice.

I could tell it threw him off.

"You said you love me, this is real, why not get

married?" I continued as I felt my power coming back to me.

When I was with Tae he had the power. I wasn't the strong, independent bad bitch the streets knew me as anymore. I was changing to be this perfect woman for him. I was becoming weak and the deeper I fell in love the weaker I was. I had lost myself; but I was determined tonight to find myself again.

Tae didn't answer me. He sat up and stared at me. When he moved his body back away from me the moon light was directly on me and he could see my entire face now. I tried to look sincere and in love now that he could see me good.

The music continued to play as the silence grew between us as *Beyonce's* remake of *Bootsy Collin's I'd Rather Be With You* filled the awkward feel between us.

"Where this comin' from, Juicy?"

I was Juicy again; go figure. I sat up in the bed because I knew that when he called me that he was almost on to me in some way. Street recognize street. I knew he was catching on to me in some way, and just like I wouldn't admit I knew what he was on; he wasn't going to either.

"I jus' thought that since we were in love maybe

we could move forward. That's all."

"Un." He side eyed me.

"What?" I tried to sound innocent.

"I haven't even met your son yet and you talkin' 'bout marriage?"

I didn't know what to say then. I almost wished I didn't say anything because I was stuck. I knew it was no way out of this and if I said anything else he would for sure know I knew who he was to Tiffany. It was obvious he was no fool.

I moved closer to him and kneeled in front of him. I looked up at him seductively as I licked the head of his member. Nothing. He didn't move, he didn't jerk; nothing. I continued to lick on him and slid his flaccid penis in my mouth and tried to suck it back to life; nothing.

I was nervous. I felt myself getting warm because I was afraid of what he might do. I was more afraid of what he was thinking right then. I sat back away from him and moved closer to where my gun was. I didn't make any movement to give him a reason to think I was going for my gun, but I needed to be closer to it just in case I had to because I didn't know what he was capable of right now. Any nigga that doesn't get hard when *my* lips touch them was either gay or on somethin' and since

I knew he wasn't gay, he was up to somethin'.

"What's wrong?"

He stood up and walked to the other side of the room and turned on the light as he looked for his clothes. I didn't say anything because I really didn't have a clue what to say so I watched him and tried to look as if I were sad he was leaving as I watched him dress.

"You leavin'?"

He glanced over at me as he slid on his Prada tennis shoe on one foot and then back in the direction of where his other shoe was as he slid it on. My heart started to pound and I almost felt as if the music wasn't on he would have been able to hear it. I reached over by my bed and grabbed my robe and slid it on.

I wasn't going to ask him to stay because if he did stay then I wouldn't have a chance to think, but a part of me thought maybe to keep the act going I should ask him to stay.

"Don't go." I said quietly.

He stood up and stared at me. His silence scared me more than anything. Whenever you can get a nigga talking then you can feel them out; but a nigga that's quiet, you have absolutely no control over and you have no choice but to expect the unexpected.

Dead silence. The music stopped and there wasn't

a sound except our breathing. Mine was heavier than his was and he seemed so calm; almost too calm as we stared at each other. I knew then he knew I knew who he was and things were about to get bad.

"Bye Juicy." He said as he paused and waited for me to respond.

When he said bye it wasn't like when he usually leave; it was more like a real goodbye, this is the end. For some reason it hurt me a little to hear him say that. I know what we had was all premediated on his end and it wasn't real, but it felt real. It felt genuine, but I couldn't let it go on. I couldn't trust him and now that he knows that I know; he can't trust me either.

He knew I knew what he meant when he was saying goodbye to me when a tear escaped my left eye. He walked over to me and took his right hand and wiped it off my face. He leaned in and kissed my lips and I returned the kiss.

When he pulled back and walked to the doorway I started to follow behind him, but didn't. I knew it was time to let him go. It made me wonder what he was going to do next because if he was leaving me alone this easy and who he was really after if it wasn't me and I realized it was Black just like Tiffany said.

I lay back on my pillow looking at the ceiling; wide

awake wondering who I really fell in love with and what Black could have possibly done to him that he went to these extremes to find him. I heard his car pull out of the driveway and I grabbed my cell phone to shoot Tiffany a text to let her know about Tae.

He knows. Was the only thing I put just in case someone besides her saw the text. I turned over on my side and gripped my pillow as I cried myself to sleep. It was just me and DJ again and I had no choice now but to go back to the Juicy I used to be.

Black

I couldn't stop Aariona from screaming as she gripped my hands and crying at the same time. I was speeding taking her to the closet and best hospital they had in Akron; Summa St. Thomas Hospital.

I was hoping that I would have been done with everything I had to do in Cleveland so we could have been back home to have my son, but he had other plans.

"I don't want to have my son here!" she yelled as her grip tightened on my right hand I swerved between cars to get her to the ER.

I ignored her and focused on the traffic in front of me. When I got back to the hotel after Tiffany shot at me, I started to tell Aariona about everything including the baby Tiffany says is mine, but when I got there all we did was argue. I think she argued herself into labor.

I released the grip she had on me and reached for my phone to call my mother. I've seen women in labor and I wondered if Aariona was really in pain or being dramatic. Either way it was driving me crazy.

"Yeah." She answered on the first ring.

"Meet me at Summa St. Thomas Hospital in Akron."

"Damn, why she screamin' like that?" she asked.

"Right." I said and hung the phone up.

I pulled in front of the ER doors as the man came with a wheel chair to help her out the car.

"Devon!" she screamed as she sat down in the chair. "Where are you going?"

I shook my head. "To park the car, babe. Go in I'm comin'." I tried to be cool.

"No!" she yelled at the nurse who was pushing her wheel chair. "Don't push me, I want to wait for my husband!"

I shook my head because the nurse looked irritated by her so I hurried to find a spot before she irritated the whole staff. I was surprised at how she was acting seeing how she was a nurse herself.

We were finally settled in the room and they had her hooked up to IV's and had given her an epidural to relax her and ease her of the pain. I was sitting in a chair next to the bed when my mother walked in.

"Hey." She said as she went straight to Aariona's side which took me by surprise since she was so adamant that this wasn't even my son she was carrying.

I really didn't want to be here to be honest because I've never had good experience in hospitals; it always ended bad in some way.

"Hey." I said as I gave her a head nod, but never

moving from my seat.

"How far is she dilated?" she asked as she rubbed Aariona head fixing her hair.

I shrugged. I didn't know what none of that shyt meant and I wasn't going to pretend like I did. All I wanted was to see was my son. My mother shook her head at me.

"How you feelin'?" she directed her attention to Aariona.

"Better now." She said softly.

The phone Bishop gave me started to vibrate in my pocket. I looked at it and silenced it and put it back in my pocket. It started to vibrate again. My mother gave me a look as if to say ignore it, but I answered anyway.

I got up to leave the room because I didn't want him to know where I was. "What?"

"I hear you back in Cleveland, Lil' Brother."

I rolled my eyes. "Stop callin' me that shyt. We ain't brothers, homies; none of that shyt!" I tried to keep my voice down as I walked down the hallway.

He paused for a minute. "Did you forget we had business to talk about?" he asked ignoring what I said.

"Nah. I ain't forget. I'm dealin' wit' somethin' more important right now. I'll be there tho'."

"Today right?"

"I'll try. I'm busy. I'll get wit' you tho'." I said as I hung up and headed back to the room. I don't know why he was in a rush to die because that's all I really came back to Cleveland for was to kill him.

I was only out the room five minutes and when I got back she was in labor. My mother was on the right side of her holding her leg and a nurse was holding the left. I stood there watching my wife's pussy expand as a small head with hair was making his way through. She was screaming with agony.

I couldn't move. I stood there with my mouth wide opened. I had never seen no shyt like this before. I was on a visit seeing my mother when DJ was born and never got to see him come out so I was in shock. Everything around me went deaf to my ears. I watched her open up more as my son slid out.

"Would you like to cut the umbilical cord, Mr. Jones?" the doctor asked.

I was stuck and was staring at my son laying on my wife's stomach then back in the nurse's arms.

"Mr. Jones?"

"Huh?" I gave him my attention.

He handed me some long ass weird looking scissors and asked me to cut the cord. I cut the cord and handed them back to the doctor and walked directly over to where my son was.

I couldn't take my eyes off of him. I watched the nurse clean him up as she talked to another nurse who was writing down what she was saying.

"8lbs 7oz 22 inches." She called out. "Born 6:52 p.m."

"Baby Jones is adorable she said to me."

"Solomon." I said still staring at him.

"Solomon?" she repeated.

I nodded, never giving her any eye contact.

"What a powerful name. Solomon." She said as she continued to write.

I tuned the entire room out and it was like it was just me and him in there. He was beautiful and had a head full of hair. He was still light, but had a dark color by the ears so I knew he was going to be my color. He didn't make a sound yet, but was breathing normal. I was crying staring at him. So this is what a child that comes from *me* looks like.

"Devon…" I thought I heard my mother faintly call my name while I was stuck in a trance.

"Devon! Oh shyt!" she screamed frantically.

"She's losing blood… get everyone out the room!" I heard the doctor yell as I turned my attention to them.

"What?" I paused. I looked over at Solomon as I

watched the nurse take the incubator he was in and move it to the side.

Aariona was laying there with her eyes closed with her head rested to the left on the pillow. At first glance she looked as if she was sleeping peacefully.

"Aariona…" I said as I walked closer to her bed side.

I looked at my mother then back down at my wife. "Wake up…baby, wake up! You did good baby, get up and see our son." I said as I leaned in closer to her tapping her face and shaking her gently.

I looked back up at my mother and she was crying. I had never seen my mother cry, ever; even when she and my father had issues or when she went to jail. Never. So I knew then this was bad. I looked at Aariona and her face was pale like she was sick. I can't believe I was so struck by Solomon I didn't pay her any attention.

"I need the room cleared!" I heard the doctor yell again as more doctors rushed in with more machines.

One of the nurses tried to calmly walk me away from the bed. I pushed her off me and she stumbled back.

"Get off me! What's goin' on?" I yelled. "Aariona get up!"

I didn't know anything about hospitals, but the sound I heard as more doctors rushed in the room made me direct my attention to the machine making it and I knew what that sound was just from movies.

"Oh my God!" my mother screamed as she covered her mouth and backed up.

My heart stopped when I saw the lines that were wavy at first go straight and then for the first time I heard my son cry. My body went numb as doctors and an officer lead me and my mother out of the room and the door closed in my face.

They rushed us down the hall to the waiting room and my mother fell to her knees crying.

"Oh God! Oh God!" she wailed.

I still was in shock. "Is she gone?" I asked the officer that was still waiting with me.

I knew he was only right there so that I didn't go back down to the room. He looked as if he could feel my pain.

"She gone?" I asked again.

"I don't know." He finally answered me in a low voice. "I do know that she does have the best doctors working with her." He said trying to comfort me.

My mother continued to cry. "God *please*! *Nooo*!"

I stood there staring down at the room she was in.

"Let me go back, please. She need *me*. I know I can make her wake up." I begged. I never begged any man for anything ever in my life, but I begged this time for her. "Please."

"I'm sorry." He said as he stood his ground.

I felt my legs give out under me and I fell into a chair. I looked up at the ceiling and started to pray.

God, please, please don't take her from me. Please. I swear I will change my ways if you just let her live. I need her God. My son needs her. Please God let him meet his mother. Please.

Tears started pouring down and I joined my mother on the floor realizing that what was happening right now was real. My mother leaned over next to me and cried louder. I knew by the way my mother was crying my wife was gone.

I knew I had lost her and she wasn't coming back. She really was in pain and she kept trying to tell me and I thought she was just being dramatic. I replayed how I was treating her and I started punching the floor where I was sitting. This can't be happening.

Tiffany

"What you doin', Bae?" I asked Key as I was riding down Superior Hill.

"Chillin', what's up?" she sounded as if she were half sleep.

"Wanna meet at the lake and smoke wit' me?"

"I'm game." She sounded excited. "Where you at now?"

"In EC."

"Fo' what? We don't know nobody over there." She asked sounding curious.

"Tryin' to find that club called Prive'. I'm thinkin' 'bout goin' to one of they Wavy Thursday's the been talkin' 'bout on Instagram."

"Mmm. Ratchet City is what they shoulda named it."

I ignored her as I hit the bottom of the hill and sat at the stop light and looked around. "You headed out?"

"Yeah. Meet you in 15."

"Bet."

As I drove further down Superior and got closer to 110th I couldn't help but to look down the street and reminisce about how we robbed them and could of gotten away without anyone knowing if Juicy wasn't confessing her sins to Black.

I was starting to wonder if I even should go through with scopin' out new niggas to rob with her because she was weak now and the more she dealt with my uncle the weaker she was becoming.

I pulled up to the lake as cars were starting to exit. This was my favorite time to come here; I wanted to see the sunset and relax.

I sat in the car rolling my blunt as I continued to glance back and forth at the sun going down. I looked at the time and she was late as usual so I put my blunt on the back of my right ear and decided to wait for her on the bench closer to where I could look at the water.

About 10 minutes went by before she pulled up and hopped out the car eagerly to get to me. I was sitting on the top of the bench with my legs rested where you are supposed to sit down at.

As she walked closer to me I admired her beauty. She had on a long strapless black sundress and some Michael Kor slide on sandals. I could tell she didn't have on any panties by the way her fat juicy ass kept eating the dress. Her hair was in a wrap and she didn't have on any jewelry except some large hoop earrings. She was dressed simple, but she was noticeable. Point blank; my bitch was bad.

I on the other hand had some distressed knee length jean shorts on with a white tank and some all-white Air Force Ones with my hair pulled in a tight pony tail. If anyone was looking at us she would probably without a doubt be considered the femme in our relationship.

She hopped up on the bench on my right side and kissed my cheek.

"Hey Baby." She said with a huge smile.

On instinct I looked around to see if anyone saw us. I still wasn't comfortable with being out in the open as a couple yet. Cars were leaving still and no one paid us any mind.

I knew we had about an hour and a half to chill before the police came and told us the park was closed. They usually sweep Gordon Park, which was around the corner from where we were first and hoped that the large rats that lived in the rocks scared us away before they had to come tell us to leave. We were from the gutta tho' so gutta rats didn't scare us.

"I got so much shyt to tell you." I said as I felt my cell phone vibrate.

She took the blunt from my ear and lit it up and inhaled as I checked my phone. I had a few missed calls and text. I never text anyone because I always felt like that was evidence people could use against you so I never thought about checking them.

"What's up?" she asked as she exhaled.

I noticed one from Juicy so I opened hers first ignoring Keyona for a moment. *He knows* it read. I frowned my face as I read it and tried to think what she could be talking about so I checked the date and time she sent it and realized it wasn't Black she was talking about, but my uncle. My eyes widened and I gave a silent gasp to myself. I knew he would be coming for me soon.

"Tae? What you doin' here?" I heard Keyona say.

I looked up and there was my uncle walking closer to us. I immediately swiped left on the messages and deleted them and quickly put my phone in my pocket. I felt my heart pace pick up slightly when I paused and realized Keyona said his name and I directed my attention to her.

"Tae?" I asked confusingly and really was about sick of this nigga knowing everyone I had contact with. "How you kno' my uncle?"

"Uncle?" she said as she frowned her face.

"Key don't tell me you fucked him too!" I blurted out.

"Fuck all that, Tiffany! You betraying me now?" he yelled interrupting her before she could speak.

"Huh?" I tried to play dumb to see how much he knew.

"You heard what the fuck I said! You told that bitch about me!"

I knew he meant Juicy and I was livid. I tried to look out for her and she runs back and tell him what I told her ass? I swear hoes be dick whipped.

Keyona tried to plead her case because she could see I was pissed at her.

"Bae, I swear we never fucked." She said grabbing my arm. "It's nothin' like that at all."

"What's it like then?" I asked.

"He asked if I wanted to make some money awhile back and I said yeah, but we never fucked. I swear."

"How did you make money? What he have you do?" I asked as I cut my eyes at him the back to her.

I wondered if that was why she fucked Black cause he sent her to get info just like he sent me and then it dawned on me that she was the *real bitch* he claimed he had replaced me wit' 'cause I wasn't movin' fast enough for him.

"Um.." she hesitated.

"Um WHAT?" I snapped.

"Remember when Juicy got robbed?"

My eyes got wide and I shook my head as I pierced my lips together. I don't know why I was mad because I didn't even like Juicy then. I wasn't sure if I was mad that it was her that did that or the fact that she kept it from me.

"What about Black?" I needed to know.

She looked confused. "What about him?"

Tae started laughing and I looked over at him. Before I could speak he punched me on the left side of my face. Not hard enough to knock me off the bench, but enough where I could feel it.

I immediately jumped off the bench and Key followed. She wasn't dressed for a fight, but that didn't stop her moving when I moved.

"What the fuck, Tae!" she yelled.

He didn't look her way. "I couldn't figure out why you and Juicy got so cool at first, but the more I thought about and watched I knew it ain't have shyt to do wit' that baby!"

I stood still and barely breathed. He had figured out what we did. I don't know how, but he did; and I wasn't going to admit to him.

"It was you and her that robbed them niggas!" he finally blurted out. "You been 'round here spendin' money, buyin' shit; wearin Gucci tank tops and shyt like a nigga won't notice!" he yelled as he grabbed the strap of my tank. "They fall off you come up? It's obvious as fuck!"

The fear I had when he first got there had subsided. I didn't speak as I observed him and wondered what his next move would be. I knew he didn't care about family enough to spare me now that he knew I went behind his back and did what I did.

I took a deep breath as I tried to process everything. It was all happening so fast and I was speechless right now. I looked him up and down with my eyes and noticed he had on all black and my eyes stopped at his hands and he was wearing black gloves.

I knew my time had come to an end and I looked over at the sun as I watched it disappear into the water. Teonna popped in my head and I was thinking how I was glad Black knew about her now so when my time was up he would be able to get her; if my Uncle didn't get to him too.

There was no fear in me, no emotions; just quick flashbacks of my life in my mind right now and I was ready to face my destiny. I looked away from the water and back at him. He stepped closer to me.

"Where is my money?" he asked.

He spoke as if he was the one we kicked in doors

and robbed personally. I didn't answer him. I didn't blink or show any signs that I feared him at all. He was looking at a mirror right now and he knew it. He smirked and quickly pulled a gun from out of his pants from behind his back and pointed it in my face. I expected that so I didn't budge.

"You think I'm playin'?" he asked.

"Do what you gotta do." I challenged him.

Our eyes were staring at each other waiting for the other one to blink. He was looking for me to break and I wouldn't. I refused to. He gave a side grin and turned his gun to Keyona and pulled the trigger.

The bullet hit her in the middle of her chest so fast she couldn't even scream. I lost my breath for a minute as I locked eyes with her. A small gasp escaped my lips as tears rolled down her face.

"Why?" she whispered as she fell to her knees.

I fell to mine to catch her and laid her on the ground. I quickly put both of my hands on her chest to try and stop the bleeding but it was coming through my fingers like a faucet running water.

"No." I whispered as tears started to fall faster. "Please don't die on me, Key. Please!"

"It hurts." She said as she went in and out of consciousness.

"I want my money." He repeated without any emotion in his voice.

I never looked at him I just kept holding her wound praying it would stop bleeding. He began to walk away. I saw him throw the gun about five feet from me.

"You might wanna get outta here. I got that gun from *your* car." He said as he continued to walk to where he parked.

I can't leave her. This ain't right. It ain't right.

I stopped crying when I realized she was already gone. It was nothing more I could do for her. My heart stopped. I didn't physically kill her, but in a way I did by challenging him. I knew what he was capable of, but I thought he was coming there for me; I never seen this coming.

I kissed her lips and laid her head down on the ground gently. "I love you." I whispered.

I jumped up to look for the gun he tossed. When I found it I looked it over and it was my gun. Sneaky bitch. He knew he was going to kill her and make it look as if I did.

I ran to my car and jumped in and sped to the freeway. I looked at my hands as her blood was starting to dry on them. My shirt and shoes were covered in her blood. I started to cry harder. I didn't know where I was going or to who I would go to because Keyona would have been the one I run to when something happened to me. I was alone and I felt lost.

The night was clear, but through my tears it looked as if I was driving through a thunderstorm. I was driving for about 10 minutes and knew the only place I could go now is to Juicy; if he hadn't killed her already.

Juicy

"I'm comin'!" I yelled out as someone banged on my back door.

I was in a deep sleep and the pounding scared me. I hadn't slept too well since Tae left me the other night and someone would pick this time to wake me. I looked at the clock; 10:34 p.m. I shook my head as I peeked through the window to see who it was. It was Tiffany.

I opened the door. "Girl why-" I stopped mid-sentence when she walked in crying covered in blood. I looked outside behind her and when I didn't see anyone I slammed the door and locked it.

She stood there crying loudly I couldn't make out what she was saying. I was scared she had Black's blood on her because the last time we talked she told me how she shot at him and I know him; he don't let *shyt* slide. You do something to him he *was* coming back; whether it be tomorrow or a year from now, you *are* going to pay for *whatever* you did to him.

"Please…please slow down." I could barely speak.

She stopped and tried to catch her breath. "Keyona is dead!"

My eyes widened. *She killed her girlfriend?*

"Tae killed her. Right in front of me." She stopped

crying and stared like a light bulb went off in her head.

"It's your fault!" she screamed at me.

I was lost. "What?"

"Bitch if you wouldn't have told what I told you about him!" she screamed and right behind that she swung on me with her right fist.

She swung so fast and I know from the way the air came with it I can tell she gave it her all. I ducked back and dodged when her left followed and caught me in the jaw.

I understood she was hurt right now, but an ass whooppin' in my *own* house I wouldn't take. I charged at her and knocked her down on the floor. I sat up on top of her to pin her down and attempt to calm her down but she was able to wiggle her right hand free and started to punch me repeatedly in my jaw. She hit me at least three times before I blinked.

I knew this was her adrenalin and I was trying not to take it personal, but the last hit got to me. I let her arms free and started to punch her in her face until she calmed down. Left first with the right following right behind.

We went for blows for about 10 minutes; neither one of us backing down from the other until we both eventually got tired.

I fell off top of her and laid next to her trying to catch my breath as I noticed she was doing the same thing.

"I didn't tell him anything." I said between breaths. "I swear."

She looked at me then back to the ceiling and broke down crying again. "She gone man; she dead!"

I felt bad for her. I couldn't believe Tae killed Keyona. He was so different from who he had pretended to be all this time. I sat up and looked at her.

"But why her?" I asked. "What she do?"

She sat up and started to examine herself. She was covered on her dead girlfriend's blood. Her shirt looked like it used to be white. She had dry blood on her face so I could tell he killed her right in front of her from the way the blood looked like it was splattered.

"It wasn't her. He was trying to break me. He knows that we robbed Bishop and them."

My eyes got big. "How?"

"I don't know. I thought you told him."

I shook my head. "Why would I tell him that?"

She shrugged. "I don't know. You told Black."

"No, he figured it out when he saw you over here."

"That's what he claimed too."

I couldn't believe what I was hearing. I was sure no one could figure it was us. I wondered had Bishop caught on too if Black and Tae did.

"We gotta kill Tae." She blurted out.

"*We?* Now, Tiffany I know you beefin' wit' him right now and I know how we met he was on one, but he didn't do anything to me at all. I'm sorry for your loss and all, but when he and I broke up it wasn't on bad terms and I do still love him."

She cut her eyes at me. "Listen you dumb dickmatized Bitch!"

My eyes widened and I was ready to fight again.

"Who the *fuck-*" I started.

"I'm talkin' to *you!*" she interrupted. "It was *fake*! The *whole* relationship was fake! I don't care what he lied and told you; it was FAKE!"

I know the relationship was fake, but *no one* could convince me the way he felt when we were together was fake. I shook my head sticking to my beliefs.

"It was so fake he was the one that robbed you!" she yelled out to convince me.

My heart dropped. I knew she was telling the truth. I knew it wasn't a lie. I felt it. I didn't say anything as I recalled that day and tried to remember everything that happened.

I looked down at the floor as I remembered it was a man and the more I thought about it, he did kind of sound like Tae, but I was hit so hard in my head I couldn't really make it out. I wondered to myself if that is why Tae always felt familiar to me; I knew his voice.

Then I remembered it was a woman there too as I looked up into Tiffany's eyes. I squinted because I did remember the female saying that she gave me what she been wanting to give me after she hit me in the head and at that time she and I was beefin' heavy about Black.

The more I thought about the more I realized she was the one that told me at the abortion clinic that she knew who robbed me and now I find out that she related to the nigga? What a coincidence.

"What?" she asked as she caught how I was staring at her.

"You right. We gotta kill him." I said without letting her know I figured out she was with him when he robbed me.

"He shot her with my gun. What am I goin' to do?" she started crying again.

"Where is she?"

"At the lake." She said as she shook her head while more tears followed. "I had to leave her there."

I stared at her not feeling sorry for her anymore.

She was shady just like I knew and she deserved every bit of what she was feeling right now.

"We gotta get you cleaned up." I got up and went to my bed room to grab her something to put on.

I came out and handed her a t-shirt and jogging pants. "We gotta burn these clothes."

She nodded.

"I'll get you a towel and make the couch up for you. Go take a shower." I said as I reached for some garbage bags to put her bloody clothes in.

She nodded without saying a word as she went in the bathroom. I wanted to kill her myself right then. I couldn't believe I fell for everything. She was a slick bitch I had to admit; but I was slicker. She was gonna get hers and I was gonna give it to her.

Black

I stared at Solomon through the window at the hospital where all the babies were sleeping. He had been here for all of eight hours and already I had his first heartbreak to prepare him for.

I leaned my head against the window hating God and everything about Him right now. I couldn't catch a break for shyt. I told Him if he let her live I would change my ways, but He ignored me.

I didn't know what I was going to do without her. I needed her and so did my son. She was the breath of fresh air through all the bull shyt. I didn't even know women could die from having a baby. I couldn't describe the pain I was feeling inside.

I felt my mother come put her hand in the middle of my back, but I never took my eyes off Solomon.

"She told me she didn't want to have him here." I started. "I didn't listen. I should have taken her back home when she asked." I started to blame myself.

"It's not your fault." My mother assure me.

She was lying. It was my fault. I hadn't paid my wife any attention because I was so focused on killing Bishop.

"Why did you tell me I was sterile?" I needed to

know.

She didn't answer me.

"Solomon looks exactly like me."

"He does." She agreed.

"And the other baby? What about her? Is that why you didn't kill Tiffany? Cause the baby look like me?" I asked as I finally turned to face her. I had to look her in her eyes and know why she had been doing the things she doing.

She backed away a step. She could see that I was serious and she couldn't get out of this one like she did with other things I asked her about.

"Yes. She looks like you too."

I dropped my head. "Why did you tell me I'm sterile then? Cause apparently I'm not!" I yelled at her.

My voice echoed and an older nurse looked in my direction and shushed me. I nodded because I didn't want her to have me kicked out of the hospital.

"I need you to be focused on what we had to have done. You were so weak. Weak for Aariona, and that's okay. I understand, but you have to know when to separate it."

"Bull shyt. Straight bull shyt." I snapped. "You saw that I had a woman I loved and you ain't like it!"

She frowned her face. "Whoa, now listen here

nigga, you ain't my man you my fuckin' son!" she began as she pointed her finger in my face. "You can fuck, love, marry every bitch in the world and I wouldn't care! Now I was told that you may not be able to have kids; that wasn't a lie."

I eased up. I wasn't mad at her; I was just pushing my anger at her because I had no one else to right now.

"I'm sorry."

She nodded and dropped her finger.

"Mr. Jones?" the doctor that delivered Solomon interrupted.

"Yeah?" I asked wanting to punch him in his face. This was the first time I seen him since he put us out the room hours ago.

"I wanted to speak with you about your wife." He said as he looked at the chart in his hands.

I didn't say anything.

"Well she had lost a lot of blood during the birth of your son which caused her to have a seizure. Did you know she is epileptic?"

I shook my head and then hesitated. "Wait, whoa." I put my hand up. "Did you say *is?"*

I had to be sure I heard him right.

He nodded. "Well yes." He looked confused.

"Wait, she alive?" I asked to make sure we were

on the same page.

He looked confused as he nodded slowly. "Well yes, you thought she didn't make it?"

I nodded as I felt my heart race and a smile came across my face. "I saw her die….. She didn't die?"

"Not on my watch. We were able to get her heart beating again and I wanted her to rest and wait until she was stable before I let you see her. Childbirth can be hard on a woman's body."

I looked at my mother and she covered her mouth in disbelief. I didn't wait for him to finish I pushed him out the way and ran down the hall to her room. I stopped at the door and opened it slowly.

When I walked in the room she was sleeping. She didn't have any tubes hooked to her just monitors and an IV in her arm. Her face wasn't flushed anymore and she was just as beautiful as she was the first day I saw her.

I leaned in and kissed her lips softly. Her eyes opened slowly and she smiled.

"Where were you?" she asked quietly.

"With Solomon."

"Where is he?" she asked looking around the room.

"Take it easy." I said gently pushing her back to lay down. "I thought I lost you." I admitted.

She shook her head. "I ain't goin' nowhere. God knows I need to be with you and my baby."

I smiled. *God*. I looked up and thought to myself. *So you do be listenin'.*

"Go get him. I want to see him."

I nodded. "Give me a minute, I want to sit with you for a little bit."

I wasn't ready to leave her side yet. I sat next to the bed and we didn't say anything at all. I just held her hand as she dozed off to sleep.

My mother came to the door and looked in, but never came in. She smiled at me and nodded. I knew she had a loving side and I was happy to see it finally.

My phone started to vibrate and it was Bishop. I took a deep breath and hit ignore. I gave my mother a look and she knew what I meant by it.

Ok God, I know I told you if you let her live I would change my ways, but it's just one thing I have to do before I change.

∞

I pulled up on the corner of Hayden where Bishop told me to meet him at. It was about four in the morning and I was tired. I had been up 24 hours straight right now and hated I just left my wife and son in the hospital; but I had to handle my business.

"I don't see nobody." I said to my mother on the phone as I looked around. "Jus' a bunch of bandos."

"He in one of 'em. I don't know what his faggot ass up to, but kill him the minute you see his ass." She instructed.

"Man, I can't be sloppy wit' the shyt, Ma. You know that."

"Yeah I know. I jus' pulled up on Woodworth. Ain't nobody 'round here either."

"Where yo' strap?"

"In my lap, where else?" she said sarcastically.

I laughed.

"We should come back when they don't expect us, man."

"They don't expect *me*. They expect to see *you*."

"You know what I meant, Ma."

"Yeah, well I want Stalyce."

"She locked up."

"Nah, she ain't. She was released." She corrected me.

I was confused. "How the fuck she pull that off?"

"The bitch a snitch, how else?" she snapped.

"That's crazy man. Yo' best friend tho'?"

"What's crazy? Her son was yo' best friend and he snaked you." She reminded me.

"Yeah, but he was jus' fuckin' my bitch. That ain't nothin' compared to what she did."

"Don't matter now. Its water under the bridge."

I was tired of waiting for him and started to pull off and then I saw him pull up. "He here."

"Who wit' him?" she eagerly asked.

"Nobody." I said surprisingly. "Call you back." I said hanging up on her.

I got out of the car and stood in front of my car as I waited for him to walk closer to me. He was parked in front of me, but about another car distance away.

"What took you so long?" I asked as I looked to see if he had his gun or anything showing.

He didn't look like he came for prepared for anything but to talk, but I wasn't letting my guard down anyway.

"Why here?" I asked when he didn't answer the first question.

"Why you ain't tell me you was here?" he asked as he crossed his arms and stood directly in front of me.

"I had shyt to handle." I said shrugging.

"How we gon figure out who robbed us?" he asked getting to the point.

"Ain't *nobody* rob *me*." I reminded him.

It took everything in me not to kill him right now, but I knew I was going to get my chance. He needed me and he wasn't trying to hide that he did.

"But, I been findin' out shyt." I added.

"What you find out?"

I wanted to tell him how I figured it out that it was Juicy and Tiffany, but then I thought about DJ and my supposedly daughter.

"I'm still piecin' shyt together." I lied. I needed to buy more time to think of somethin' else.

"They jus' found Keyona dead at the lake by Gordon Park." He said changing the subject.

I raised my eyebrows and my jaw dropped as I folded my arms. "Damn."

"Somebody blew a hole in her chest." She said shaking his head.

"That's fucked up."

I decided to use that info to my advantage. "It's fucked up 'cause that's who I found out robbed you." I said lying.

His eyes got big. "What the fuck you mean? She set it up?"

I nodded.

He shook his head. He wasn't buying that. "Nah

that don't read."

I shrugged. I knew it didn't sound right and I knew he wasn't going believe it. I wouldn't have. I still can't believe that it was Juicy and Tiffany myself, but I couldn't let him go after either one of them.

I wondered what Bishop would do to Juicy if he knew it was her now that she was the mother of *his* child. I really wanted to get all this over with and go back to Miami.

"I hear yo' mom home." He said.

I didn't like the way he said it. It sounded like he was up to something; more like an indirect threat.

"Yeah, I hear yours is too." I said making sure he knew to read between the lines.

He nodded because he understood what I was saying.

"How she out tho'?" I asked out of curiosity.

"Good ass lawyer." He said smiling.

"I bet."

"I got some shyt to handle; meet up later?" I asked. I really wanted to get back to the hospital.

He nodded. "Seriously, Black."

I nodded and got in my car to call my mother. "Tell Stalyce I said what's up." I said through the window as I pulled off.

I knew he was going to try and follow me so I drove around St. Clair for a while then finally hopped on the freeway by Eddy Road to head back to the hospital.

"What he say?"

"Nothin' for real. Aye remember that girl Tiff was kissin'?"

"Yeah."

"Somebody killed her he said."

"What? When?"

"I don't know. But he said they blew a hole in her chest."

"Damn."

"I'm headed back."

"Aight. I'll see you there later."

I knew she wasn't going to rest until she found Stalyce so it was no point in talking her out of it.

"Be safe, Ma."

"Yep." She said hanging up on me.

If I knew her like I thought I did she was following Bishop since I left him.

Tiffany

Young girl murdered in cold blood whose body was found at the lake has now been identified as 19 year old Keyona Whittaker…..

The news was talking about Key as I sat there on Juicy's couch watching and crying. I had been at her house since I came over the other night.

This shyt hurt so bad. I hadn't even been home to see my daughter and every time my mother called I would rush her off the phone. I knew now that Key's body had been identified she would be calling me soon.

Juicy walked in the living room and cut the TV off and stood in front of it with her arms crossed.

"We gotta figure out somethin'." She said with an attitude.

"Figure out what? I can't even think straight!" I yelled as I threw my hands up.

"I don't know, but you can't keep sleepin' on my couch!" she snapped. "You ain't seen your daughter. Yes it's fucked up how Keyona died, but your daughter needs a mother!"

I just stared at her. She was right. I couldn't keep sleeping on her couch. I needed to find my uncle and kill him. I don't even think he cared about the money for real, I think he just likes the power he has over people. He couldn't get me to fold on his own so he killed her to make me.

I really didn't want to leave Juicy's house because that meant that I would have to face reality. I thought about where Keyona could have kept her part of the money so I could steal it and give that to my uncle.

I knew it wouldn't be enough, but I would hope at least it bought me some time to think of how I could get him back for killing her.

My cell rang and it was my mother just as I expected.

"Hello." I finally answered after her calling back to back three times.

"Tiffany! Where are you?" she yelled frantically. I could hear Teonna crying in the background.

"Over a friend's house. Why is she screaming like that?"

"Did you hear about what happened to Keyona?" she asked as I heard her voice began to crack.

I started crying again silently. "Yes." I pushed out through tears.

"Oh my God!" she began to cry too. "Do you have any idea who would do that to her?"

"No." I lied.

How could I tell her that it was her favorite brother?

Her own flesh and blood killed my best friend right in front of me without even blinking. How can I tell her he enjoyed watching the blood drain from her body until she was completely lifeless?

"Tiffany, you have to know *somethin'*....you two were too close for you not to know *anything*." She wouldn't let up.

She was right. I did know. I knew everything. I knew it was all my fault she was gone too and her asking me only reminded me of it and I hated her for it.

"I said I don't know! So stop fuckin' askin' me!" I shouted and hung up on her.

Juicy was standing in the doorway of the living room watching me with her arms crossed shaking her head.

"All *that*," she said as she waved her right hand in a circular motion toward me, "is gone get you caught up in the blame for her murder. You sound suspect as fuck."

Juicy was right. I knew that it didn't sound legit or even believable that I didn't know anything about her or her dying because we were inseparable. We were so inseparable that I knew the police would be coming to question me soon and I knew I had to get myself together before I ended up the blame for her death.

"You right." I said as I wiped the tears from my face and stood up and stretched. "I'm 'bout to go."

"Where?"

"Home."

"Okay." She said nonchalantly.

"Do you know how I can get in touch wit' Black? I really need to make sure if things go left soon that he takes his daughter."

She shook her head.

"I figured. If he stops by, please give him my number."

She nodded.

From the way she was responding to me I could tell something was wrong or she was just tired of me being in her house so I followed her queue and left.

I sat in my car and really didn't know where to go. I didn't want to go home because I would have to deal with my mother's questions, but realized I had no choice but to get it over with.

I took the long way home trying to gather my story together to keep me from looking like I was anywhere near her when she killed.

I couldn't focus as I was driving because I kept seeing the moment replay in my mind as if it just happened. I could hear the sound of the gun shot and how it sounded when the bullet pierced her flesh echoed in my ears. I cringed at the thoughts and started to cry again.

Get it together Tiffany.

I pulled in the driveway and sat for about ten minutes before going in. The house was quiet when I walked in and I was glad because I still wasn't prepared to talk to my mother. I went up to my bedroom and Teonna was laying in her crib sleeping.

I stood over her crib and stared at her. For the first time since she was born I felt like I loved her. I wanted to pick her up and hug and kiss her, but she was sleeping so peacefully I didn't touch her.

Tears began to flow again and I couldn't control it. I have never cried like this before. I never felt this kind of pain before. I contemplated on if I should just take my daughter and go to college or something; maybe enroll in one of those programs for single mothers.

"Hey." My mom said quietly as she walked up next to me and watched Teonna sleep.

I wiped my face because I didn't want her to see me crying. "Hey."

"How you holdin' up?"

"I'm not." I admitted.

She grabbed me and hugged me. It felt foreign to me because she never hugs me, but I needed it right now so I embraced it all. I laid my head on her shoulders and let the tears flow.

"Why did he have to kill her Ma?"

She paused for a minute. "Who baby?"

I wanted to tell her so bad and I almost did, but the doorbell rang before I could.

"I'll be right back." She said as she rushed down the stairs to get the door.

I wiped my face and looked out my window and saw police cars; about four of them. I frowned my face and wondered what was going on. I knew they would come ask me questions soon, but not that many of them. I glanced in Teonna's crib and she was still asleep so I went downstairs to see what was going on.

"Tiffany?" a man in a suit asked.

"Yes?" I replied confused.

"I'm Detective White. I need you to come with me to the station. I want to talk to you about your girlfriend Keyona Whittaker." He said politely as he showed me his badge.

"Girlfriend?" my mother asked. "They were just best friends." She corrected him with a disgusted look on her face at the thought of her being my girlfriend.

He glanced at her then back to me and I dropped my head because I didn't want to tell my mother the truth.

"Come with me, please." He asked again noticing the reaction I had to what she said had to have been something she didn't know of.

"Is she in some kind of trouble?"

"Well there was a murder and she is our prime suspect."

"What?" I asked confused as to why I would be the *prime* suspect or even a suspect for that matter.

"What the hell are you talkin' about? That girl was like family! She wouldn't hurt her!" my mother screamed in my defense as she moved in between myself and the detective.

"Well she can come to the station and give her statement and she can explain the bloody clothes." He said as he looked me in my eye; never once looking at my mother.

"Bloody clothes?" I asked with my eyes widened.

He nodded and it dawned on me; Juicy set me up. She said she was burning the clothes the other night and I was so distraught I trusted that she did, but never checked.

My heart dropped and I wondered why she would have turned the clothes in to the police. It made sense now as to why she was wondering where I was going when I left her house. She didn't ask out of concern; she asked so she could tell them where to find me.

"I didn't kill her." I said to the officer.

"Well maybe you can tell us who did." He said as he took me by the arm and led me out the house.

"This is bull shyt!" my mother screamed as she followed behind us.

I knew there was no way out of this right now. I could tell them what happened, but I don't think it would matter. They already believed it was me and who knows what she told them.

It was no point in crying right now because my tears wouldn't save me. I was devastated that my best friend was dead and now I was being charged for it. My life was over now and I knew it. Teonna was left without a mother now and because Juicy set me up I knew she wasn't going to tell Black what I asked her to tell him.

As I sat in the back of the police car staring out the window I replayed the last two years in my mind. I couldn't figure out how I got here or what made me fall in love with the street life, but I regretted it.

I wanted to go back to the day that my uncle came to me and asked me if I wanted to make some fast money. I still remember it like it was yesterday. We seemed closer then; as if we had a real bond.

The sun was shining that day. It was extremely hot so I wore my hair in a bun on top of my head with a pretty yellow sundress on and some white sandals I picked up from Rainbow. My skin was glowing because the sun had kissed me just right over the last few weeks. My mother decided to barbeque that day and invited over a few of family members.

"Hey pretty girl." Uncle Tae said to me as he sat next to me on the front porch.

My face always lit up when he called me that. I didn't have a father and he was the closest thing to a male role model I had. My uncle wasn't the friendly type and everyone in my family wished that he would talk to them more. He had more money than all of his siblings and had no problem flaunting in front of them. He only gave my mother money and attention because she was his favorite and because I was her child he showed me love too.

"Hey Unk. What's up?"

"Where yo' money at?" he asked flashing his pearly white smile.

I shrugged. "I don't got none."

"As pretty as you are you not supposed to be broke. Wanna make some money?" he didn't hesitate to jump right in. "It a be fast money too." He tried to sell me on the offer.

"How fast?" I asked because I wasn't convinced I could

make fast money without stripping or selling drugs since I was only 16.

He looked around to see if my mother was close and when he saw she wasn't he leaned in to talk. "Fast. As pretty as you are it will be easy for you too."

I still wasn't convinced. "What I gotta do?"

I wasn't worried if it had something to do with sex because I wasn't a virgin and I knew a few things when it came to the bedroom.

"All you gotta do is make yourself noticeable to this dude; flirt, make him like you; seem like you like him, find out where he stay, gimme the info and I'll handle the rest."

I stared at him wondering what was next, but he said nothing at all. He stared back waiting on my response.

"That's it?"

"That's it." He said with a smile.

I twisted my mouth to the side wondering what the catch was. "Mmm. Do I gotta fuck him?"

"You might. That maybe the only way you find out where he stay at. Or get him to think he gon' fuck, go back to his place and pretend you on your period or some shyt. Whatever you gotta do to get the address."

It sounded too easy. "How much I get paid?"

"Ten."

My eyes widened not believing him. "Ten what?" I

needed to hear him say it.

"Ten thousand."

I was a 16 year old girl who shopped at Rainbow and Shoe Time for fits because that's all my mother could afford and he just told me I could make 10k just to find out where a nigga lay at night? I was all in. I was so ready to give him any address he needed. I would be paid for doin' nothin' but my usual.

"I'm in." I said without hesitation.

He smiled at me. "My girl. I'll tell you where to be later on."

"Okay."

"And you can't tell nobody 'bout this okay? Not even your closest friend." He said sternly as he looked me in my eyes.

I nodded. "Okay, Unk."

"I'll tell you where to be tomorrow. You might have to skip school for a day."

"Okay." I shrugged.

Skipping school was something I did for free whenever I didn't feel like going or going to see my dude; so doin' it for 10k wasn't a hard choice.

He reached in his pocket and handed me some money. Here's a thousand to get you started. Make sure you dress sexy."

I couldn't believe he gave me that much money. I had never had a thousand dollars before and I couldn't stop smiling.

"Thanks Unk!" I said staring at the money feeling rich.

It all seemed so easy in my head as I thought about it all night. I could barely sleep I was so excited and I wondered who the nigga was. I hoped he was cute because it would be a lot easier to get him to like me if he was. It was hard to fake with a ugly nigga.

The next day I made sure I put on my tightest jeans and shirt to show my curves and some wedges with my toes out. I had pretty feet and didn't mind showing them. I looked down at my nails and frowned. If he was a dude with money like my Unk said he would never look my way with these chipped and brittle nails.

I rushed out the house and headed to the bus stop to hop on the Rita…(that's what we called the RTA public bus transportation in Cleveland) to catch the 50 across 116th to Buckeye Plaza to have the Chinks give me a quick full set.

I was excited about having hundreds in my pocket. I felt like I looked like money as I switched off the bus and walked down to the plaza. As I was walking so many niggas was stopping trying to shoot there shot at me, but I would smile and turn them down. I was loving the attention; it felt good to be noticed.

Then there was this one guy; he pulled up in a black Escalade with rims. We locked eyes, but he didn't try and talk to me. He watched me as I walked to the nail salon and I stared back at him. We never broke the stare, but our eyes were talking to each other. He was fine as hell. I wanted to forget about who my uncle sent me for and jump in his passenger seat.

Before I reached the nail shop he motioned for me to come to his truck so I did. I was nervous and anxious at the same time when I reached the window of the driver side. I wasn't as tall as the truck window so I couldn't lean inside like I wanted, but my wedges gave me a small boost.

"Where you goin'?" he asked with a half-smile.

"Get my nails did." I said with a huge smile as I slid my hands in my back pockets so he couldn't see my nails.

"Let me see em."

I shook my head still smiling. "Wait til they done."

He paused and leaned his head out the truck and looked me up and down then at my feet a little longer and sat back in his seat.

"Pretty feet."

"I know." I said with a side grin.

"What's your name?"

"Tiffany. Yours?"

"Black."

I paused and stopped smiling as big. Black? No this can't be the same one my Uncle wants to set up?

"Black? Where you from Black?" I asked to be sure and hoped it wasn't the same one; I never had a description of him, just his name.

"Down the way." He said lying.

I was happy when he said that. This wasn't the same one I was looking for then. I decided to take his number so I could talk to him after I was doing what my uncle asked me to do.

We talked for a minute; exchanged numbers and parted ways. After I got my nails done I hurried home to wait for my uncle to call. I couldn't stop thinking about Black and his smile. The phone rang and broke me out of my fantasies of he and I.

"Hello?"

"You ready?" My uncle asked me.

"Yup. Ready as can be!"

"Good. Okay I told you his name was Black right?"

"Yes."

"He usually hangs out in The Valley; that's where his BM Juicy stay at."

"Okay. What he look like?"

"Dark skin, about 6'2" maybe 6'3"; not a cocky nigga but he ain't little either."

"Braids? Dreads?"

"Nah, he keeps his hair cut. Waves I think."

"What he drivin'?"

"He got a few cars. Sometimes whippin' a old school Monte C; but lately I seen him in a black Escalade."

My heart stopped and I knew I had already met my "job". "A what?"

"Black Escalade; it's a truck." He explained.

"I know what it is." I snapped.

"What's the attitude fo'?"

'I jus' met him." I said in a low voice and disappointed that it was him.

"Where?"

"Buckeye plaza. I was goin' to get my nails done and he tried to holla."

"Damn! See I knew you was the right one!" he sounded excited while I was upset and couldn't share the same enthusiasm.

"Yeah." I said dryly.

"So what happened? You didn't turn him down did you?"

"Nah. We supposed to hook up this weekend."

"Even better! The shyt started off natural so it will make this easier! Damn! It's a go!"

"Yeah, you right. Imma lay down for a minute, I don't feel so good."

"You not getting' sick are you?" he sounded worried.

"Nah. Cramps." I lied.

"Oh okay. Hit me when you get up so I can tell you what to look for when you meet wit' him."

"Okay." I said and hung up the phone.

That was the first day to the turn around of my life. I went from a regular 16 year old girl to a woman with experience of many men bunched into one.

"Watch your head." The officer said as he helped me out the back of the car.

They didn't handcuff me yet; which told me they did have me as a suspect, but they could possibly let me go if my story was what they needed to hear to close me out as the killer.

I walked through the police station scared. I wasn't so much as scared for me, but for Teonna. Just when I actually wanted to change it was too late.

I sat down in the room where they were going to question me. I had seen this so many times on The First 48 and wondered if they had the same feeling I felt right now and if the fear that I felt right now is what made them snitch.

They left me in the room alone for about 15 minutes and I sat there thinking with my head hung down what could I possibly say that would help me become free.

I could hear the line of questioning in my mind now; *who killed her? My uncle Tae. Why? Uh because we took over the robbery of local drug dealers that he had planned first because we wanted to keep the money for ourselves. Who are the local drug dealers? Uh, my daughters father, the nigga I was cheatin' on him for and they friends. Oh and it was my gun he used.*

The whole scene was fucked up when I ran it down in my head and screamed that I should be the headline of *Dumbest Criminals.*

I couldn't figure out a way to make sure I didn't go down for her murder without telling on everyone that I knew; so I chose to be quiet. Whether that is the right choice or not, I'll have to find out.

"So you want to tell me what happened at the lake?" the detective said as he sat in front of me with a yellow legal pad and a manila folder.

I've seen many interrogation shows and I knew off top there were photos of the crime scene of her in there and I prayed that he didn't show me them. I couldn't take seeing her like that again.

I knew they didn't have anything in my phone to go off of because I never saved anything at all in there. No text, no pictures, emails, voicemails; nothing.

I didn't answer him I just kept looking down at the table in front of me.

"C'mon Tiffany. I know you were there with her. Your phone call to her before she died and the bloody clothes you were wearing tells me that you were."

I looked up at him with my eyes, but left my head hanging down. We stared for a brief moment and I stayed silent then resumed my focus back to the table.

My silence wasn't to protect Tae at all; I could give a fuck about him right now. My silence was to protect myself. I knew anything I said could be incriminating to myself.

The detective quickly grew tired of me not saying anything and wasted no time. He snatched the manila folded and began throwing her pictures in front of me one by one. Huge 8x10's of my best friend; my girlfriend.

"Why'd ya' kill 'er?" he asked. "Huh? You two had a lovers quarrel? She said somethin' to piss ya off?"

I said nothing.

"What was it? Was she gonna leave you?"

Silence.

"Or did she threaten to tell your mother about you two and you were afraid mommy wouldn't accept you bein' a little carpet muncher, huh?" he continued.

I lifted my head and cut my eyes at him. He was

way off base and I wanted to punch him in his mouth.

"Yeah, that's what it was." He said as he smiled and eased back into his seat like he was waiting for an award like he had just solved a mystery.

"You don't know what the fuck you talkin' 'bout." I snapped.

"She speaks!" he shouted.

I shut my mouth and looked back at her pictures laid in front of me. They must have found her right after he killed her because the pictures had captured the blood looking fresh. I started to cry as I softly touched one of the pictures.

"Damn." I whispered. She was really gone.

"What happened!" he yelled as he smacked the table in front of me.

Silence.

"Fine. Have it your way."

He gathered the pictures in front of me and slid them back in the folder. He looked at the officer that had been silently standing in the corner watching us the whole time and signaled with his head to cuff me.

The officer immediately walked over to me and I stood up. I didn't fight it. It was no reason to because they gave me a chance to confess what happened and I didn't so fighting it would have been pointless. I slid my hands behind my back and stared at the detective with a blank look.

"You have the right to remain silent..." he began.

I smirked to myself because I had already used the fuck out of that right. As he finished and led me to where he was taking me to do the processing I couldn't stop thinking about how I was going to be known for killing the one person I loved more than anything in this world and I had no way out of here to come after her real killer.

I was allowed one phone call and I badly wanted to use it to call one person and one person only; Juicy. I had to know why.

Juicy

I was pacing back and forth across my living room wondering if my theory on Tiffany robbing me with her uncle was right because I knew there was no coming back for me turning in her clothes to the police.

When I first came up with the idea I didn't have a doubt in my mind it was her; but for some reason I keep feeling like I may have been wrong in the pit of my stomach. I felt it so deep that it almost made me sick.

My cell rang and I noticed the number right away. I had so many people call me from the county for years that I knew it was her. They must have believed me or else she wouldn't be calling me right now.

You have a collect call the operator began; I knew the drill so I accepted the call immediately. I wondered what she was going to say to me because I know for a fact she knew it was me that gave them her clothes. No one else knew about the clothes *but* me.

"Juicy!" she started in attempting to whisper slightly but frantic at the same time.

"What?" I asked nonchalantly.

"Why the fuck you do *me* like this?" she asked still talking low.

Talking low or whispering didn't matter and I knew

that because calls were monitored and since she hadn't been sentenced I knew they would most likely be monitoring hers.

"You did this to yourself." I said calmly.

"Yo', all I did was look out for you. I didn't expect this shyt from you." She said as her voice began to crack.

"Look out fo' me? You think I ain't remember it was *two* people that came to my house last year?" I said not mentioning in detail because it was a jail call.

"Huh? What the fuck you talkin' 'bout?"

"The other night? I realized that it was *you*!"

"Me? Juicy I ain't have shyt to do wit' that! I had jus' found out that same night I told you!" she yelled and then began to lower her voice.

We both became silent.

"There was a female there. That's who hit me."

"I know and my hand to God it wasn't me."

I believed her. She sounded serious as she could sound and I didn't even have to look in her eyes to know she was telling the truth. I felt my stomach get weak as I felt like I wanted to throw up right there. I sat on my couch and grabbed my stomach with my left hand.

"Oh my God." *What have I done?*

"What about my daughter now? Huh? You had this speech this morning about how my daughter needed me, but you the one have me lookin' like I did some fucked up shyt and *you know* I ain't do this shyt!"

"I have to go." I said in a low voice.

"What am I supposed to do?" she asked desperately.

"I don't know."

I didn't know what to tell her. I hadn't a clue at this point on what I could even do to help her out. I would have to have Tae come over and figure out how to make sure the police knew it was him, but he was way too smart for that and I knew it.

I knew when he told me goodbye the other day I probably wouldn't see him again and the reality of it was that Tiffany was going to jail for what he did and it was my fault. I ended the call without another word. I honestly felt bad right now.

∞

"So how long does it take to get my results back?" I asked my OBGYN as I sat up straight on the table.

Never giving me eye contact as she sealed the swabs she just took from my vagina. "A few days. Not long."

I made an appointment to get checked after Bishop raped me. I knew I should have come sooner, but it began to hunt me that he been sleeping with men for God knows how long.

"I'll call you with the results. I don't see anything visible right now. How many sexual partners do you have?" she asked writing on her chart.

I only had one, but because of the rape I knew I had to say otherwise.

"Two." I said in an embarrassing but low voice.

That caught her attention because she glanced at me the right back to her file she was writing about me. I wanted to scream right now. I felt humiliated as this elderly white woman was judging me in her head and the thought of what Bishop was out here doing sickened me. I felt like he was better off dead somewhere.

I got dressed quickly sliding on my leggings and tank and headed for my car to rush and pick DJ up from Bishop. I really didn't want to see him right now and I hated the fact that my son had to be around his gay ass. When I got to the car I checked my phone and he had already called my cell five times and there was one call from a number I didn't recognize so I called back immediately.

"Hello."

I didn't recognize the voice.

"Somebody call Juicy?"

"It's Peaches."

I paused. I didn't expect to ever hear from her again and I really didn't want to talk to her after what I did. She really loved my son so I was ashamed to face her.

"Hey." I said wondering if this was about to be our blow out.

"I need to talk to you."

"Look, Peaches, I'm sorry 'bout what I did-" I began and she quickly interrupted me.

"Stop. I'm not callin' for that. Where can you meet me at?"

I was puzzled. "Well if you ain't callin' 'bout that then what you want wit' me?"

"I jus' need you to meet me. Ok?"

"Okay. Now?"

"Yes."

"Where?" I couldn't imagine what she would want with me.

"Jus' come out to 260th."

"Why so far?"

"Call my phone when you get here." She said and hung up before I could respond.

I started to call Bishop back, but decided to wait to find out what Peaches wanted since my curiosity got the best of me.

All kind of thoughts went through my mind about what she wanted with me. I wondered if she knew about the baby Tiffany had and if she had found out about the set up on Black. I hoped she didn't because I knew she would show no mercy when it came to him.

I pulled inside of some apartment parking lot so that I could call her phone and see where to go from here. I hadn't seen her since our last visit a year ago.

"Is that you in the red Audi?" she asked as soon as she answered.

"Yeah." I said as I looked around to see where she was.

"Thought so. Here I come."

I sat my cell on the dash board and wondered who stayed out here. I knew it wasn't her because Black wouldn't ever live in Euclid. He said it reminded him too much of the hood so I was almost positive he would have her somewhere else too.

As she walked toward my car I noticed how hard she looked and walked. She had her hair back in a sleek pony tail like she always wore it when I came to visit her in jail. She had on a men's white tank; we called them wife beaters, some jeans that had a few slits by the knees and some all -white Air Force Ones. If I didn't know any better I would assume she switched over while she was locked up.

She went straight to the passenger side and I unlocked the doors as she hopped in. We stared at each other for a second attempting to feel the other out.

"Hey." I finally said.

"Hey. How are you?" she sounded genuine.

"I could be better."

She nodded. "DJ?"

"He is getting better."

"Bishop?"

I rolled my eyes and turned my head in embarrassment. I had fucked up what I built with Black for a faggot that I'm not even with anymore and everyone knew it. She gave a small laugh.

"I hear you been seein' Deontae." She said skipping the small talk.

I looked her way again. "How do you know him?"

"I know everybody." She said without hesitation almost like she knew I was going to ask her that.

"What about Tiffany?"

"I know her whole family. Where can I find Deontae?" she steered back to the point.

I shrugged. "I don't know." I said as I turned my head and felt myself tearing up at the mention of him.

I still loved him and I know after finding out the truth I was supposed to hate him, but part of me felt like I was supposed to still protect him because I loved him so strong.

"You know. I know you know or else I wouldn't have come to you. So cut the bull shyt." She snapped.

"Why you lookin' for him?" I was curious to what she knew.

"You know as well as I do why I would be lookin' for him. Last time. Where can I find him?"

I shrugged again. I really wanted to cry. I was tired of the game. I was tired of the streets and not knowing who I could trust. I understood now why Black just up and disappeared and nobody could find him.

Being in Cleveland living the lifestyle we lived felt like you were contemplating suicide with a noose around your neck while you tried to stay balanced on a chair and the chair you were on was falling from under you as the noose got tighter and tighter just suffocating you slowly day by day as you tried to stay alive.

"What you want from me, Peaches?" I asked as I stared her in the face.

I had nothing left to give. I didn't even want to give anything anymore. I was done; tapped out.

"I need you to bring him to this hotel room I'm

going to give you the key. Seduce him. Do what you do, just make sure he is weak and tired however you need to. Then leave the room and leave the rest to me."

I couldn't control it any longer; the tears poured down my face like a leaky faucet. She was going to kill him and I knew it. I didn't want this.

"You owe my son." She reminded me.

I dropped my head in my hands as I cried uncontrollably.

"You owe *your* son." She said as she pointed at me this time in my face.

I knew I owed DJ for taking Black from him. He didn't deserve that and no matter what Black did to me he didn't deserve it either.

I wiped my face and sat straight up. "Okay."

She smiled a half smile.

"Today."

I turned to her quickly. "How?"

She shrugged.

"He not dumb. He not goin' for that and we jus' broke up."

She handed me a key card and a piece of paper.

"Where is this?"

"Broadway. Right off the freeway. Jus' take him to the motel and I'll do the rest."

She didn't wait for me to respond; she just hopped out of my car and left me there.

He would never go to a place like this. I would have to think of something else or a different place. I tried to get myself together and make sure my voice didn't crack as I pulled off toward the freeway and called his house phone. If he was there I would be shocked.

Ring. Ring. Ring.

House phones seemed to ring longer than cell phones and then I realized why he never had a cell phone after finding out what he really did.

"Juicy?" he answered as if he was happy, but surprised I called.

"Hey." I said feeling the tears about to come down when I heard his voice.

Why can't I hate him? I know the truth, but yet I'm still in love.

"What's wrong?"

"I-I jus' miss you. I know we said our good byes, but…"

The tears came down again and I had to take a minute to calm myself. My left hand was shaking as I tried to hold the steering wheel steady.

"I miss you too."

I pierced my lips together and shook my head. My

heart believed him, but my head said don't trust him fool.

"Can we get a room?" I asked to see what he would say.

"A room?"

"Yeah. I need to be with you right now. Even if you just hold me."

"Why can't we go to your house?"

"I got Bishop over there watchin' DJ. I had a doctors appointment." I lied.

"Somethin' wrong?"

"No. No. just a regular PAP test."

The lies continued to roll off my tongue and it felt like he was buying it.

"Okay."

"Where you wanna get one at?" I asked.

"Independence good for you?"

"Yeah. I'll meet you in 30."

"Juicy?"

"Yea?"

"Don't come on no bull shyt." He said sternly as his voice changed to a voice I never heard before.

He sounded like he knew I could possibly be trapping him into something; but yet he needed to see me as bad as I said I needed to see him.

"I'm not. Jus' want it to be us for a little while."

"See you in 30." He said as he hung up on me.

I turned off the freeway on Eddy Road to head to a hair store. I had my gun with me, but I needed to get a blade just in case Tae was the one who came on some bull shyt. The gun would make too much noise; but a blade would slice a nigga up 20 times before he knew it.

I made sure to hurry because I didn't want him to be suspicious of me being late. He made it to the hotel before I did and called me from the room.

"Yeah?"

"Room 210."

"Okay."

I was glad he got there before me because it allowed me to go in the back way and not be seen. I stood in front of the room door for a minute trying to get my breathing together. I was nervous to see him after all that has happened the last week.

He must have felt my presence or knew I was close because he opened the door before I could knock.

Tae stood there holding the door open in nothing but his black Polo boxer briefs and the smell of his Gucci by Gucci cologne hit me in the nose and sent a feeling through my body that made my knees weak almost immediately. Tae had the sexiest body I ever seen and I loved every inch of it.

"Come 'ere." He commanded.

I obeyed and went straight to him as he grabbed me closer and let the door close and kissed me so passionately. I closed my eyes and hugged him so tight as we kissed allowing each other to just enjoy the moment. It was like the other shyt was nonexistent right now; like everything was just right.

When he held me I felt safe. I knew he was a monster when he was out in the streets, but when he was with me he was different. It was like I was the Beauty and he was the Beast and I was the only one who could tame him.

He tightened his grip as he took his right hand fondled my breast and began to kiss on my neck making my *kitty* drip. She was awake and it was all because he awoke *her*.

"Tell me you love me!" he whispered in between kissing my neck.

I closed my eyes and leaned my head back. "I love you!" I moaned as he moved his right hand from my breast slowly down my body and slid into my leggings.

As soon as he touched me down there my body jerked and I grabbed him to secure my grip because I was getting weaker. He laid me on the bed and used the hand that was inside me to pull my leggings off.

I glanced at his member as it was protruding through his boxers and seeing it so hard for me turned me on. He stood at the edge of the bed and licked my juices off his fingers. I bit down on my bottom lip as I watched him slide his boxers off.

I sat up and took my tank off and threw it. I didn't have on any underclothes when I went to the doctor. We both admired each other's body for a few minutes and then he slid onto the bed face first in between my legs. He didn't bother to kiss my thighs like he usually does and tease me; he went straight for my clit.

He moved his tongue in and out of me; up and down; in circles teasing me; making my body jerk until he made my love come pouring down in his mouth as I screamed his name while tears of ecstasy came out simultaneously. He buried his face deeper as he licked and slurped every drop. My legs trembled until they fell down; no longer able to hold themselves up.

He smiled as he crawled on top of me and positioned his body over me holding himself up in a push up position; I smirked and looked up over my head at him and slid the head of his member in my mouth and flickered my tongue over it teasing him as he began to jerk.

Our eyes locked as he began to rock his hips as he

went slowly in and out of my mouth. I let the saliva build up so that he could start to go as deep as he wanted. It turned him on when he was able to fuck my mouth and never once felt my teeth scratch him at all.

I started to take control as I slid my tongue up and down his member; letting it go in and out of my mouth; switching up the rhythm as I would tighten my grip with my lips and then I slowly slid my right hand around the base as I jacked him off as I slid back until just the head was on my lips while I softly tongue kissed it then slid underneath it so that I could lick his sack softly while I continued to jack him off with the lathered saliva I left on his member as I softly massaged my clit with my left hand to keep me ready for when he entered me.

He let out a loud moan and fell to his knees and I stopped everything immediately.

"No, Daddy….don't cum jus' yet." I whispered as I turned over underneath him and lay flat on my stomach. He leaned back on his knees and smacked my ass.

"Ah!" I yelled with pleasure in my voice.

He took both my ass cheeks and spread them apart as he slid inside me slowly. I loved this position.

I felt him moving slowly and he took his left hand and gripped the back of my neck and smacked my ass again with his right hand.

"Ahhhhh! Damn! Daddy! Awe shyt!" I screamed as I gripped the sheets.

He leaned in and grabbed my hair and started to move deeper and slowly on my G-Spot. My body jerked. He always knew how to make me have multiple orgasms.

"Don't stop!" I begged.

"Deeper?" he panted.

"Yes!"

"Say it!"

"Deeper, baby! Deeper!"

I didn't have to say no more; he went deeper and I felt myself explode as he came with me. He grabbed my hair as he came and yelled out my name, *Oh shyt Juicy, got damn!* As he collapsed on top of me and our bodies became one while he tried to catch our breaths.

"Damn, baby."' He whispered as he moved my hair to the side so he could kiss my neck and face softly.

I closed my eyes to enjoy the moment. I didn't want us to get out of this bed and leave this room. In this room we were in love; we were happy. When we left this room it was curtains for us.

He got up and sat on the edge of the bed and I leaned over and reached in my purse to grab my cell phone to see if Peaches or Bishop called me; and they both called a few times a piece.

I sat my phone back down and scooted up on the bed behind him putting my legs on each side of him as I hugged his back. To my surprise he took his left hand and put it on top of my hand while they were locked around him.

We were silent as we listened to the air condition in the room and each other's breathing.

"You know we gotta talk." I broke the silence.

"Yeah I know."

"Why?" was all I asked to see what he would confess to me.

He broke our lock we had and moved away. I leaned over to him and pulled him back toward me until his head rested on my left thigh. He allowed himself to relax as he stared at the ceiling.

"It's a lot you don't know." He began.

"Why me though?"

"It wasn't personal. It wasn't even 'bout you."

"Who was it 'bout then?"

He glanced up at me then back to the ceiling.

"What we had….what we have….is real."

I believed him. No one could make me think otherwise because I know what the chemistry is between us.

"Who was it 'bout then?" I wanted to see how far he would go in telling me the truth.

"You different. When I'm with you, I'm different." He ignored my real question.

"Why you want Black so bad?" I had to ask because I see he wasn't going to tell me anything on his own.

"A long time ago….his father took somethin' from me…..it doesn't matter now."

"What he take?"

"It doesn't matter now." He repeated.

I knew he was going as far as he wanted with that story so I went to my next question.

"Why did you rob me?" I asked as I felt tears coming.

It felt strange asking the person I just gave my entire mind and body to this question.

"It was jus' business." He said coldly.

He said it like this was the part of the game I was supposed to respect. I silently let the tears flow as I reached up and wiped my face and slid my blade out of my mouth.

When I reached to check my phone I was able to grab my blade and slide it in my mouth without him noticing because his back was to me.

"Business huh?" I wanted to be clear.

"C'mon Juicy. You know how this shyt goes.

"Yeah I know. You do too, though. You know in *this* game you get what you give."

He was still calm and laid back while we were completely naked. In this hotel he wasn't as nervous as he usually is. Usually he is on guard and alert at everything around him, but right now he was at peace. He relaxed like he felt complete trust between us.

"Yeah." He agreed.

"Tae?"

"Yeah?"

More tears silently crept down my cheek. "No matter what, I love you." I whispered.

He looked up at me as he was on my thighs and with a quick flick of my right wrist I slit his throat back and forth about 3 times.

I heard a gasp for air as he paused like he didn't know what just happened to him. He took his left hand and began to rub where I slit him at as the blood quickly filled his hand.

I leaned back as I cried some more watching the man I love die in front of me slowly while still laying on my lap.

"I'm sorry baby, it's not personal." I whispered as I leaned in and kissed his lips.

I had seen plenty of people die growing up in The

Valley, but this time it was different. It hurt more than anything to do this to him, but I knew I could never be with him after learning the truth no matter how good the sex was or how intense our connection was.

His eyes were bulging as he held onto his neck with both hands now like he wanted to attempt to stop the bleeding himself. His blood continue to pour like a waterfall as it ran down behind him and saturated the white sheets.

He couldn't speak or scream and he wouldn't stop staring at me. I knew then that the look he had would be embedded in my head forever and would haunt me in my dreams.

After about ten minutes his body finally went limp and his hands fell to his side while his eyes remained open looking in my direction. The blood continued to ooze and I took my hand and closed his eyes.

I slid from underneath him and walked to the bathroom crying as I ran my shower water. I looked in the mirror and began to cry harder. I had never killed anyone before and I didn't know what would happen next. I wondered if I would be on my way to jail with Tiffany. I just murdered the person that the police needed to set Tiffany free.

I took a long shower as I washed away his semen

coming out of me and his blood off my thighs. The water ran red for about ten minutes before it finally became clear.

I wrapped the towel around me as I went to call Peaches. I couldn't stop staring at him lying on the bed still bleeding.

"Where are you?" she answered immediately.

"Independence. Come to the Comfort Inn in Independence, room 210. Come up the back way."

"He there?"

I didn't answer her I just disconnected the call as I stood over the bed staring at my Love realizing he would never get up again. The tears stopped finally; I was drained from the sex, crying and killing him. I was officially a murderer.

I walked over to the side of the bed and slid my clothes on and began to go through his pockets to see if he carried any I.D. or something to tell me more about him. I found the keys to his car and a wallet.

I sat in the chair in the corner as I went through his wallet and there was a Magnum condom; something we never used and pictures. I pulled them out and there was one of me folded up behind his insurance card. Then there were professional wallet sized photos of three kids; two boys and a girl. I knew immediately the bigger kid was his; he was the spitting image of him.

My heart sank. Who was he? I didn't even know who I was really dealing with. The next picture was of a white woman by herself. It appeared to be from the same photo shoot the kids were in. She was gorgeous. She had full lips and wide eyes and her make-up was flawless; it only enhanced her beauty while her perfect smile was the icing on the cake. She looked happy.

I turned the picture over to see if she had written anything on it and just as I suspected she did. *For my wonderful husband. The last 13 years have been wonderful and I can't wait to spend the rest of my life creating new memories as we grow old together. With you by my side there is nothing I can't accomplish. Love your wife, Terri.*

I squinted my eyes at his dead body. I wanted to get up and slice him up some more. He was *married*? He had a whole family ducked off somewhere and I never knew or even had a clue. I wondered who she thought he was because as far as Tiffany made it seem he was just a hood nigga robbing other hood niggas like Omar from *The Wire.*

I threw the wallet down and looked for the key the room as I grabbed his car keys so I could go see what else he was hiding. I slid on my sandals quickly and headed back out the back way and went to the parking lot to look for his car.

I didn't even see the car he usually drove so I began to hit the alarm button on the key chain until I heard his car go off. My eyes followed where the sound was coming from and it landed on a dark blue Volkswagen with tented windows.

I silenced the alarm and headed to the car as I looked around to make sure no one saw me. I never seen him drive this car before, but I realized it's a lot I never knew about him.

I sat in the driver side of the car quickly looking through everything. I don't know what I was looking for; I was just looking. Nothing was over the visor. The car was pretty spotless and I looked in the glove compartment and found a cell phone and a car title.

The title read *Terri Foster* and the address it was registered under was Canton, Ohio. He didn't even live in Cleveland; but an hour or so away. I shook my head. I took the cell phone and began to look through it reading text messages between him and *Terri*. I had to know how he pulled this off.

Their conversation was pretty boring as I waited for his IMessage to "load more" of their text. My eyes stopped as I laughed when I read her ask him what did he want to eat after church or if he wanted to eat out.

Church? This demon went to church? Go figure.

Then I came across what I really wanted to know; he told her he sold two houses that week. So she thought he was a realtor. Which would explain how he was able to tell her he was in Cleveland so much. He was the true definition of living a double life.

I wiped the phone down with my shirt and put it back in the glove compartment as I rushed to go back inside to see if Peaches came. As soon as I hit the back steps where the exit was she was already there headed up in front of me.

"Hey!" I called out to get her attention.

She turned and waited on the top step for me. "Where is he? He suspect anything?" she asked.

I shook my head as I continued in her direction. "He don't expect shyt."

She smiled. "Good."

We looked around as we headed to the room keeping our heads down in case of a camera and walked in the room. She reached behind her back pulling out a gun with a silencer attached and I didn't say anything I just allowed her to walk into what she was too late to do.

She paused when she peaked around the corner to where the bed was and her eyes landed on the crime scene. The gun slowly dropped as her bottom lip followed and she moved closer to the bed in shock.

There was so much blood since I left the room that you couldn't tell the sheets used to be white. The sympathy I had when I first killed him had subsided as I learned who he really was. The only sympathy I had was taking him away from those kids.

"Juicy." She said softly.

I joined her right side and stared with her. "Yes?"

"We gotta clean up all traces of you."

"Okay."

"Put the do not disturb on the door."

"Okay." I said again still not moving.

"We gotta move fast, Juicy."

"Yep."

I couldn't move for some reason. I wondered why I knew and attracted so many deceitful people in my life. Is it because it's true that you attract what you really are and not who you want to be?

"Now, Juicy."

I began to move when she said that because I knew time was running out. I looked for the do not disturb sign and hurried and slid it on the door.

She turned and faced me. "Now we gotta clean up everywhere you touched and look for strands of hair. The sign should buy us some time and they might not find him for a few days."

"Okay." Was the only response I had for her.

There was nothing more to say. I trusted that she would make sure I got away with this and that we were now even. I killed the man that started the havoc in our lives and that was for sure was to redeem me from what I did to her family.

She nodded and walked in the bathroom as I followed.

Black

"I'm ready to go home." Aariona blurted out.

I knew this was coming soon and I was hoping that she would have held out until I was finished with what I came to do. I continued to stare at Solomon and without answering her hoping she could see now wasn't the time. Of course she didn't take the hint.

"I should be at home with my baby in *his* room. Not this hotel!" she shouted as she threw the baby blanket off of her and jumped up and went into the kitchen area.

I continued to hold my son while my eyes followed her as I watched her stomp around mumbling and pouting. Any other time it would have irritated me, but after the death scare in the hospital it made me laugh to myself. I'd rather have her mad right now than not be here at all.

"Chill, Baby."

"I don't want to be here!" she yelled.

I gave her a serious stare. "Don't wake my son up."

Her eyes widened as she gasped in shock. "Oh! *Your* son?"

"Enough. This is goin' too far. You know what we came here for."

"I don't even care about that anymore! I just want to

be home in Miami!"

I laid Solomon on the couch and walked over to her and pulled her close to me and hugged her as tight as I could.

"We goin' home; soon. I promise. But you gotta let me handle my business."

"I'm scared." She started to cry as she tightened her grip on me. "What if something happens to you?"

I laughed. "Girl do you know who I am here? Ain't nothin' gon happen to me."

She pulled away from me and wiped her face. "Don't start that shyt, Devon! Nobody is invincible; not even you!"

I shook my head. "I'm goin' to do what I came to do, Aariona."

"What about Solomon?" she asked as she folded her arms.

I knew she was going to play that card and I was already prepared for it.

"What 'bout him? Were you worried 'bout him when you asked me to come kill Bishop? Because our son was there then. It's not like he jus' came about."

She didn't say anything because she knew I was right.

"Listen, as a man it's my job to protect my family and

allowing that nigga to do what he did and still breathe makes me a bitch. So I'm doin' this for my son."

I waited for her to respond, but she knew it was nothin' she could say to what I just said to her so I kissed her forehead and headed out.

"I love you, Devon."

"I love you too.

Soon as I got in the car I called my mother.

"Where ya at?"

"Juicy house. Get here now."

I raised an eyebrow. "What?"

She hung up without responding to me. I wondered what they had going on so I hopped on the freeway and sped to her house.

The sun was setting and the breeze was nice for a day in September in Cleveland. Not too hot and not too cold. When I got to the side door my mother was right there waiting on me. She opened it and looked behind me and pushed me through the door and closed it quickly and locked it.

"Man, what's up?" I was confused right now but the way she was acting I knew they had to have done something.

She didn't answer she just followed behind me while

I walked straight to DJ room. He was sitting in his wheel chair watching TV.

"Hey DJ." I said smiling.

He looked up and his face lit up. "Hey, Dad!"

I kneeled down in front of him. "What you watchin'?"

"Disney Channel. Mommy keep cryin'."

"Oh yeah? Why is that?" I asked.

He shrugged. "I think somebody died and somebody went to jail."

I frowned my face wondering what he heard. "Who was it?"

He shrugged again.

"Stay here. I'm gon' find out what's goin' on ok?"

He nodded.

"And don't come out 'til I tell you it's ok. Ok?"

He nodded. I was about to close the door when he called my name, "Hey Dad?"

"Yeah?"

"When you come back can I go with you?"

"We will see."

"Okay." He said as he redirected his attention to the TV.

I closed the door and headed to the living room. My mother was sitting on the arm of the love seat dressed in all black; blank tank, black pants and black Air Max. She had her hair pulled back in a tight pony tail as usual

Juicy was sitting on the edge of the couch and she looked like shyt. Her hair was in a sloppy pony tail and was wet like she was working out heavy. She had on a black t-shirt that looked like it belonged to a nigga and some black New Balances. At first look it look like maybe they went and worked out together, but Juicy's body language told a different story.

She was shaking her right leg as she sat with her legs open and rested her arms on her legs and held her hands together tightly. Her eyes were puffy as if she were crying for days and neither one of them said a word.

"Why the fuck DJ know you been cryin' man?" I started in on her.

She didn't respond she just looked up and cut her eyes at me.

"You hear me talkin' to you?" I asked as I stood directly over her.

"Tell him what happened." My mother instructed.

"I killed Tae. She said softly as she started crying again.

"Damn. Your first body."

Because she and I had history I was concerned about how she was feeling after killing someone. I remember the first time I killed someone and how it got to me.

I was 16 years old and it was normal for Bishop and I to be out in The Valley at night hustlin' and fuckin' wit' hoes. This night wasn't normal. Nothing about it felt normal. The wind didn't even blow the same. It was like death was walking through our projects looking for his victim to take with him. The night was still and the moon was bright red. I remember because as I smoked my blunt and looked at the sky I didn't see not one cloud nor a star. The sky was completely black and the red moon shone. It amazed me; grabbed all of my attention for about ten minutes as I sat on the crate outside of Kisha's apartment.

Kisha was one of Juicy so called friends. She wanted to be like her so bad that she had to have everything Juicy had, clothes, shoes, purses, hairstyles; and me.

Kisha was bad in her own way though, so mimicking Juicy she really didn't have to do. I liked what me and Kisha had going though. She knew her place and she knew to respect Juicy and never let her know about us and I was goin' to give her what she was lookin' for whenever she wanted it.

About 15 minutes of sitting alone she came outside and sat next to me. Bishop was across the way at another apartment. Where he was I could see him and he could see me. We never did anything separate.

"Wow!" she said as she looked up at the moon.

"Right." I said passing her the blunt.

She shook her head. "You know I don't fuck wit' that shyt."

I shrugged. "More for me."

"You comin' inside?"

I looked around to see who else maybe outside to see me go inside. I was sure people knew we were doing something, but never really caught us so they didn't talk too much about it.

I went in before she did and she followed me. I went to her room like normal and took my shirt off. Everything still felt off about the night, but I couldn't quite put a finger on it.

She walked up behind me and hugged me as she rubbed her fingers softly down my chest. Her touch was always comforting so I closed my eyes and let her rub me.

"I jus' don't understand why we can't be together." She started in.

"Not tonight, Kisha."

She pulled away from me and went and sat on her twin sized bed.

"Come 'ere."

I sat my gun on the dresser and walked over to her and climbed on top of her as I started to kiss her neck. Usually I'd be rock hard when I'm with her, but even my dick knew something wasn't right tonight. I pulled back and stood up.

"I gotta go."

She frowned. "Why?"

"Somethin' ain't-"

WHOP!

Something hit me in the back of the head and I hit the floor. I reached behind my head and felt the back of my neck was wet as I tried to regain my balance.

Kisha didn't scream or say a word. She slid back onto the bed removing her feet from the floor. I tried to focus my eyes and see what she was looking at and she gave a look as if she knew who was there. I glanced behind me and my gun sitting on the dresser seemed so far away.

I crawled away from where the legs were standing behind me to see who it was as I slid my right hand in my pocket and grabbed my cell slowly. I slid it out under me as I clicked talk on Bishop's name so he could hear my background.

"He still movin'." Kisha said in a low voice.

The legs moved over closer and kicked me in my ribs a few times as I hit the floor.

"What the fuck!" I yelled out so Bishop could hear me on the phone.

He was only across the walk way, but his timing getting there seemed like hours. The legs hit the floor and I scooted away. Bishop had rushed in and pistol whipped the person who hit me in the head. Blood was still oozing from the back of my head and I stood up trying to force myself into staying conscious.

"You good, Lil' Brother?"

"Yeah." I said as I held the back of my head as I walked over to pick up my gun.

I squinted my eyes in pain from the blow to my head and walked over to the nigga layin' on the floor and cocked my gun. I looked over at Kisha as she started to cry. Her plan went sour and she was afraid.

I walked over to her and stood in front of her as she held her knees to her chest and shook my head.

"You dumb bitch." I said as I raised my gun to her face and shot without thinking a second thought.

In the moment it felt right. In the moment I was in right now it wasn't me. I didn't think about the consequences at all. All I thought was revenge. I watched her face split open from my bullet as pieces of it splattered everywhere.

"Damn." I heard Bishop say then fire two into the nigga he just pistol whipped.

I stared at Kisha for a few minutes before Bishop tapped me.

"Let's go."

We ran out the backway of the apartment and went to his mother's which was around the other side of the building. My adrenaline was still going and I noticed the wind began to blow. I saw clouds come out and cover the red moon and I could have sworn I saw a hooded shadow waiting by the door when we got to her apartment.

I stood inside the bathroom staring at the mirror for a long time. I had just killed someone for the first time, but didn't feel any remorse. Kisha was my first of many bodies.

"I'm scared, Black." Juicy said as she broke me out of my flashback.

"I know. You gon' be aight tho'." I said as I took both her hands and held my arms on top of her legs so she would stop shaking.

"What about DJ?" she asked as she sought reassurance for him as well.

"He *will* be aight."

"What happened?" I needed to know.

"I found out he was the one that robbed me."

My eyes widened and I gave a quick glance at my mother then back to her. "What?"

"Tell him everything."

"Tiffany is his niece."

"I know."

"She's in jail." She hesitated telling me that part.

"Why?"

"For killin' Keyona."

"That's bull shyt. She wouldn't kill that girl."

"She didn't, Tae did." She said looking down.

"So why the fuck is she in jail?"

She didn't answer me.

"Hello!"

"Tell him." My mother commanded again.

"Because I sent her there."

"What! What the fuck you mean *you* sent her there?" I said as I stood up and mugged her.

"I thought she robbed me wit' him!" she tried to justify it.

"So fuckin' what! If that's what you thought you handle that shyt yourself! We don't call them bitches for shyt! You know that!"

"I killed him for you too! He was comin' after you too!" she said jumping in my face.

I waved my left hand. "Nah, don't try that one! You did that shyt for yourself! That ain't have shyt to do wit' me at all!"

"If you wouldn't have been fuckin' around on me for that snake ass bitch back then none of this wouldn't have happened! I told you she wasn't shyt!"

"Bitch you fucked around on me for a faggot!"

Her eyes widened. "How you know 'bout that?"

"Don't worry 'bout it. You a snake ass bitch too."

"Fuck yo' bitch ass, Black!"

I back handed her in her bottom lip and she pulled back as she wiped the blood from her lip and calmed herself quickly and my mother jumped in between us.

"I don't know what to do to get her out of there. I fucked up." She said shaking her head as she looked down at the floor.

"Yeah you did fuck up! That's all you do is fuck up shyt! You ain't shyt *but* a fuck up!"

It must have hurt her hearing me say that to her because she dropped her head in both her hands and started to cry hard. I didn't even care.

"Okay enough you two. We need to figure out what we gon' do 'bout the baby and Bishop." My mother interrupted.

"Ma, I don't know that baby!"

"I don't give a fuck if you know her or not! She is *yours* and apart of *you* and *you will* take care of her until the mother of your child is released from jail!" she said as she pointed her finger in my face.

I knew she was right but I didn't know how I was going to tell Aariona.

"What about my wife?"

"What about her? If she loves you then she loves every part of you and that baby is a part of you. Or she can get the hell on!"

Since she was released from jail all she talked about every chance she could was about how Aariona could be gone.

"My wife ain't goin' nowhere." I said as I stared her in the eyes.

"If you have to make a choice between her and your child I trust that you will make the right choice."

"My wife ain't goin' nowhere. Period." I repeated.

"What the fuck ever!" she shouted as she walked away.

I directed my attention back to Juicy. "Where is Bishop?"

"How the fuck should I know? Probably somewhere wit' a dick in his mouth." She said rolling her eyes.

"Chill. I need you to get him over here."

"He ain't 'bout to come and I ain't 'bout to ask his bitch ass to come over here!"

"You owe me."

"I don't owe you shyt! I paid my dues when I killed Tae."

"Look, all I came back here for was him, not none of this other bull shyt."

"He not gon' come Black! He raped me a few weeks ago so he know I ain't callin' his ass for no dick or nothin' else! Okay?"

I frowned my face. The more I looked at her the more her pussy seemed tainted to me. "He raped you?"

She nodded. "I ain't fucked wit' him since we found out 'bout DJ at the hospital."

I folded my arms and looked at the ceiling so I could think real quick.

"Aye, I'm 'bout to take DJ to my room and come right back."

Juicy jumped in front of me before I could go to his bedroom. "What? Where the hell you takin' my son?"

I frowned my face. "Your what? Man you betta back the fuck up Juicy." I said pushing her back.

"Nah, you ain't takin' him nowhere Black! And he ain't goin' around that bitch!" she yelled.

I stepped closer to her face. "Get the fuck out the way Juicy. I'm not doin' this wit' you right now."

I took my right arm and moved her to the side. She attempted to push back, but couldn't stand against my strength.

I opened DJ door and walked straight to him. His face lit up like he didn't just see me a little while ago. Juicy followed, but knew how I felt about her acting up in front of him so she stayed quiet.

"Hey DJ, you wanna go wit' me for a little while? I

want you to meet your baby brother."

"I have a brother?" he said smiling.

I nodded.

"Yes."

I immediately picked him up. "Grab his chair." I said to Juicy.

She didn't say anything she just followed me with the chair and I could tell she wanted to stop me, but she knew she couldn't.

I sat him in the car and buckled him up and closed the door so I could talk to her for a second. She put the chair inside the trunk and closed it. I leaned against it and crossed my arms.

"You know this is the end right?"

She nodded and tears started to flow.

"Chill. The tears gon' have to wait 'til it's all over."

"Where are you taking him?"

"I'm goin' to let him stay wit' her where it's safe. She not like us. She different than us."

"She has your baby?" she asked looking me in the eyes.

I nodded and she turned her head away from me. I knew it hurt her to hear me say I had a wife and a son because she did deal with my bull shyt for so many years, but what I have with Aariona I would have never had that with Juicy.

"I don't know what's goin' to happen tonight, but I know this is goin' to be your last time here."

She took a deep breath and exhaled, but stayed silent while I talked.

"Get whatever you need out the house that's important and all your money. Pack you a bag, no bigger than your Louie duffle bag and put it in the trunk while I drop him off."

"Okay."

"Get Bishop over here."

"How?"

"Will he come if it's about DJ?"

"Yes. Quickly."

"Okay. Tell him that DJ relapsed and you don't know what to do and you're scared."

"Okay. Then what?"

"Wait for me."

"Black?"

"Yeah?"

"She not raisin' my son. I am."

I nodded. "Well then you know what you gotta do right?"

"Yeah."

"Collect yo' self. After this over wit' you can live a

normal regular boring life somewhere else." I said as I wiped her tears from her cheeks.

"How did you sleep at night after you killed so many people?" she asked obviously still shaken up about it.

"Who said I can sleep?"

I walked to the driver door and looked up and saw my mom standing in the doorway watching us. We gave each other a head nod and I hopped in the car.

DJ was smiling as he stared at me. "I can stay with you forever now?"

I smiled. "Your mom might miss you."

He didn't like my answer and quickly turned his attention outside the window.

As I drove on the freeway I decided to warn Aariona that I was bringing DJ.

"Hey." She answered on the first ring.

"What you doin'?"

"Watchin' Solomon sleep. Is it over?" she jumped right into it.

"Not yet. I need your help."

"With what?"

"I need to bring DJ to you for a little while."

Silence.

"Hello?"

No response.

"Do you hear me?" I asked.

"I hear you." She said sarcastically.

"Don't do that. I'm askin' you to watch my son while I do this please."

"Your son? Tuh…*this* is *your* son over here."

I got quiet for a second. I couldn't believe she said that. I didn't expect that from her especially since she knows how much I love DJ.

"This is my son too, Aariona."

"Wow!"

I knew from her response that it would be a big blow out once I told her about Tiffany baby so I decided to wait as long as possible. I hung up on her when she said wow because I didn't have time for that shyt right now.

When I walked through the door pushing his wheel chair the attitude she had prepared for me disappeared when she saw him in the chair. I knew that she wouldn't be able to say much when she saw that. Her face slowly rested as she looked as if she had sympathy for him.

"DJ this is your step mother, Aariona." I said staring her in the eyes.

Her right eyebrow raised slightly as she looked from me to him. "Hello, DJ."

"Hi. Can I see my brother now?"

Aariona tilted her head to the right slightly as she

gave a me a look to say *what the fuck?*

"In a minute. I need you to take care of her and your brother while me and your mommy go handle some business, can you do that?"

He nodded.

"I need to talk to you now." She said as she laid Solomon on the blanket on the couch.

I knew I had to make her calm down before I left and I hoped it wouldn't take too long. I walked in the room and she closed the door behind her. I turned to prepare myself for the drama.

She had her hair in a bun on top of her head and one of my t-shirts and my pajama pants. She looked so beautiful right now and right now I wanted to lay her on the bed and taste her, but the thought went away quickly when she started to talk.

"So now I'm the babysitter while you and your old bitch run the streets?" she snapped.

I shook my head. "Nah. Nothin' like that. She know a way to Bishop I can get him without him bein' prepared for it. Make it quick and easier so we can go back to Miami."

"You know what!" she started as she shook her head, crossed her arms and laughed like the crazy women do when nothing is really funny at all.

I've never seen her like this and it was kind of cute to me. "Baby, you don't have nothin' to worry 'bout." I said as I grabbed the sides of her arms.

She began to tap her foot on the floor and bite the inside of her jaw. She always did that when she was mad or nervous.

I touched her cheeks. "Stop that shyt. I don't want that girl. I want you. I wouldn't fuck up what we got for that hoe. Trust me."

She stared at me without blinking.

"I jus' want to do this and take you home. That's it. I promise."

"Devon, I need this to be the last thing. I need when you kill Bishop that you kill "Black" too."

I nodded. Whatever she needed to hear so I could go, but *Black* would never die. He will always be remembered. I kissed her forehead and walked out the room and kissed both of my sons.

"Take care of them for me, okay?"

DJ nodded and I left without giving Aariona anymore attention. It was time to finish what I came to do.

Tiffany

"So what am I facin'?" I asked the nerdy white boy sitting in front of me.

I had to accept a public defender because I couldn't trust to tell my mother where my money was at so that I could hire a real lawyer.

The one that was given to me had on some tennis shoes that seemed to have run its course and some khaki pants with a button down. He looked more like a computer hacker than a public defender.

It was crazy thinking about how all the time I schemed and plotted about the streets it never dawned on me to have a lawyer on hand. I never thought that I could actually be in jail at all. I didn't see past the glam and the fun we were having to even prepare myself for times like this.

"Well," he started as he continued to look through his paperwork never looking at me. "I'm going to be honest with you. Because you won't tell them what happened you're being charged with aggravated murder and that's maximum life without parole."

My heart paused and I felt life escape my body for a minute. *Life without parole?*

"Are you fuckin' serious?"

"I'm afraid so."

I was sitting here facing life and would be forever known for killing someone I loved more than anything in this world while my uncle was out running free probably plotting on his next victim.

He stared at me for a second. "Why won't you tell what happened?"

"I didn't kill her."

Silence fell on the room as we stared each other down.

"I believe you."

"Good because I didn't do it."

"I also believe you know who did. Are you scared for your life if you tell?"

I shook my head. It wasn't my life I feared for, but Teonna's.

"Listen, if you tell me what happened I'm sure I can find a loop hole in the law to rid you of these murder charges.

"Nah. I don't trust that shyt."

"Okay." He said without a fight as he started to pack up his things.

"Wait."

He paused and looked at me.

"I jus' want to go home to my child."

"I know I can find a way to make sure you don't go down for murder. You will do some time for what you did, whatever that maybe, but not aggravated murder."

"What I gotta do?" I was desperate.

"First you have to be completely honest with me. Then you have to tell me what happened; even your part in it. What you tell me stays between us."

I sat quietly for about five minutes and decided to do it. If it would at least clear me of murder I had to give it a shot. Life without parole? My life had just began.

"Okay. Let's do this."

He took a tape recorder out of his brief case and a yellow legal pad and after about two hours of talking and questioning we finally wrapped it up.

"So now what?"

"Now I go home and work on your case." He said as he cleaned up his papers.

"Do you think you can really help me?"

"Yes. From what you told me and after I go over the evidence again, yes. I believe this case can help you as well as me."

I nodded as the officer came to take me back to my cell.

"I'll be in touch."

It was hard to just up and walk away leaving the fate

of my life in his hands, but him trying was better than nothing at all.

I decided to call my mother before I laid down to sleep. Since I been in here all I did was sleep; hoping that I would wake up and this would all somehow just be a dream or some kind of vision like in the movies where they would see their life flash before their eyes of what could happen if they continued to live the way they lived.

Every day I would awake; even when it was a quick nap I would be quickly reminded this was no dream and I would fall into a mental depression all over again.

"Well it's about time you called." My mother started in as soon as she accepted the call.

"Hey, Ma. How's Teonna?"

"Well she doin' okay, but she been lookin' for you. She looks across at your bed every day. I think expecting to see you laying there."

I closed my eyes and shook my head at myself. "Don't do that, Ma. Don't tell me that stuff, okay?"

"Well, it's the truth."

"How's my brothers?" I asked changing the subject.

"Fine. Staying out of trouble. I been trying to get in contact with your uncle to see if maybe he can help out and find you a good lawyer but he haven't been answering my calls."

I rolled my eyes. "I just bet he haven't answered your calls."

"Now you know he loves you. He would help if I could find him."

The more she mentioned him the more I got irritated.

"Look Ma, I gotta go."

She started laughing. "Go where? Chile, you ain't goin' nowhere."

I hung up on her and went to lay down. I was so angry and frustrated with her and everything else I wanted to hit something. I did think it was odd as I looked at the ceiling that he hadn't responded to her.

No matter what went on he would come running whenever she needed him. I felt alone right now. I had no one else to call or talk to and it hurt. I turned on my side and for the first time since I been here I cried myself to sleep.

Juicy

"You gon' be ok with this?" Peaches asked me as I paced back and forth across my living room.

I packed the trunk up like Black told me too and wondered what he had in mind for Bishop. I hadn't called Bishop yet because I didn't want to sound suspect. Then it occurred to me that I didn't know why he wanted to kill Bishop too. They were like brothers and I hoped it wasn't over what I did with DJ.

"What you mean? Hell yeah I'm ok wit' it! I told you what he did to me!"

She nodded. "Yeah, but he is the father of your child and you were in love wit' him for a long ass time."

I stopped pacing and stood in front of her and crossed my arms. It felt strange that I was having this conversation with her because she and I built a bond while she was in jail because she thought DJ was her grandchild.

"Did you know that DJ wasn't Black's?" I had to know because she seemed to know a lot and kept a lot of secrets.

She nodded.

I looked away in embarrassment. "Why did you let me keep comin' every month to see you with him all those years then?"

"Because my son loved him and he had already had everything taken away from him; me, his father, his entire life. He needed DJ and bein' a father meant a lot to him and I wasn't goin' to take that from him too."

I nodded. "I respect that."

"But I thought 'bout everyday how if it came out and he got hurt behind it what I would do to you." She said sternly as she stared me in my eyes.

I wasn't sure if this was her threatening me or not or her letting me know she was going to do something to me so I stayed quiet to see what was next with her.

"But you started to grow on me after a few years so I left it alone. I figured if it hadn't come out by the time he was two then it would never come out. Shyt happens in strange ways, huh?"

"Yeah."

The room became silent as we just stared at each other until her cell rang. She never looked away from me as she answered it.

"Yeah?"

I figured it was Black so I sat on the couch and waited until she got off the phone.

"Ok." She said after a few moments and then hung up with him.

"Go head and call him over."

I nodded as I took out my cell phone. "I need to know before I call, why is he 'bout to do this? It's not cause of me is it?"

She shook her head.

"DJ?"

"Nah."

"Then why? They were like brothers and the only problem they had was *me*. So it don't make sense."

"Ask him."

"Why can't you jus' tell me."

"Cause it's not my place."

I needed to know before I called Bishop so instead of dialing his number I called Black first.

"What's up? You called him already?" he asked answering on the first ring.

"Not yet."

"What you waitin' on? I'm on my way back!" he yelled.

"You never said why you want to kill him. I know why I want to, but why do you? Is it about me and what I did?"

"Don't flatter yourself." He said calmly.

"Well what is it 'bout?" I begged to know.

"He disrespected my family."

"Your family? That bitch you married?" I yelled.

"I don't have time for this. I'll be there in 15 minutes." He said hanging up on me.

I threw my phone and screamed. I couldn't believe he was going so hard for this bitch. I needed to know who she was and why he loved her so much. He was always there for me, but not like he is for her right now and I had to know why.

I looked up at Peaches trying to calm myself down. I was breathing heavy because I was so angry.

"Who is she?"

She shrugged.

"You don't know her?"

She shook her head.

"So he jus' up and married some random bitch?"

She shrugged again. "He knows her, I don't?"

"And you let this happen?"

She frowned her face at me. "*You* let this happen. *You* had him. He was yours. *You* fucked that up and pushed him right to her. No matter how much he liked her his loyalty to you and DJ would have never allowed him to leave you. You opened that door and he walked through it."

I knew she was right and I was pissed. I know that girl had nothing to do with how I was feeling right now, but as soon as I see her I'm hittin' her in her face.

"So it's my fault?"

"You gave your man to another woman, yes it's your fault!" she yelled at me as she threw her hands in the air.

"I hope that bitch die!" I shouted in anger.

She shook her head. "Don't let him hear you say that. He is very protective over her and at the rate you goin' you losin' his loyalty and any concern he has for you altogether."

I sat back on the couch and folded my arms. I really fucked up all the way around. I knew she was right and I knew that Black wouldn't have left me for nobody no matter what as long as I stayed loyal to him.

"If he married her, he was already gone."

She nodded. "Maybe. But he wouldn't have left you."

I stared at the ceiling wishing I could just go back to redo it all over, but that never would happen. I didn't even know which way to go so that I can make the best of my life now. Everything is different now.

"Time to make the call, Juicy."

I sat up and went and picked my cell up off the floor and tried to sound scared and not so much as angry. I need Bishop to believe me.

"Hello? Where you at?" I asked after having to call

back to back a few times before he finally answered.

"Around. What's wrong?"

"Somethin' wrong wit' DJ and I don't know what to do!" I said crossing my fingers because I didn't want to jinx my son again.

"What? What the fuck you mean somthin' wrong wit him?" he yelled at me.

"It's like he relapsed or somethin'."

"Here I come." He said hanging up on me.

"He bought it?"

I nodded. "He on his way."

She nodded as she frowned her mouth down and picked up a piece of metal out her bag and began to screw it on the front end of her gun and I realized it was a silencer.

My heart began to beat fast because this was all becoming real and I felt a queasy feeling in the pit of my stomach. She could sense how I was feeling as she glanced up at me then back to her gun to continue what she was doing.

"You aight?"

"No." I admitted.

She laughed. "Hit them lamps. Leave the kitchen light on and move DJ bed against the wall. Leave that middle of the room completely open."

I didn't respond I just did as I was told. Just then Black walked in the house and straight to DJ's room.

"Yeah this will work." He said as he folded his arms.

Peaches walked up beside him and handed him the gun with the silencer. "Ready?"

He nodded. "You?"

She laughed. "Make sure you find out where Stalyce is before you kill him."

He nodded. "You cool Juicy?" he asked looking at me.

I still had an attitude about this being about his so called wife. "Can we talk for a second?"

Peaches sucked her teeth. "Let it go, Juicy."

I rolled my eyes at her and gave my attention to Black. "Please?"

"Later. We don't have time for this."

Peaches rolled her eyes and stepped inside the closet and cracked the door. You couldn't see her, but I was sure her vison of us was perfect.

I wanted to say something else, but I knew our time was limited and Black's focus wasn't on me or what I was feeling.

"Go look out for him. What time he say he was comin'?"

I shrugged. "He said he was on his way."

Before Black could respond we heard him pull in the driveway and he looked toward the driveway through DJ bedroom door then back at me.

"You ok, right?" he asked again.

"As I ok as I can be." I said trembling.

"Imma make sure he never hurts you again, ok?" he said trying to calm me.

I nodded. Black slid behind DJ's bedroom door and I heard the side door open. I took a deep breath and tried to relax my body. Here goes.

Black

I eased behind DJ's bedroom door thinking to myself how I was really about to kill someone I've known my whole life.

So many memories ran through my mind of good times he and I had. I couldn't believe all that time I was around him I didn't really know him for real. I never even had a clue my father was molesting him.

I always wondered why my mother never left me alone with him after a while or why I was always with her no matter what business she had going.

It started to make sense to me now why Bishop had so much hate in him. I remember when we would catch niggas slippin' he wouldn't just shoot them, he would torture them and I would always make jokes about him needing a hug or having a fucked up childhood. I never knew his childhood was fucked up in reality. I always thought we had pretty good lives.

I reminisced on this one time when my mother first went to jail and we had just left my father's funeral.

It was a rainy day in May. The funeral was small and quick. He didn't have any family, but us and we really didn't want to go to the funeral at all, but Stalyce made us. I thought it was awkward that she gave him a funeral when I was that young because she was the one who killed him, but then as I got older I realized she did it to keep from looking like a suspect.

She didn't give him an expensive funeral or even a real obituary; he definitely had the bare minimum.

Bishop and I were sitting on his aunts top porch looking at the rain. I didn't realize it then, but as I think about it now he was showing his feelings on his face as he stared at the rain. It was like a sad feeling, but relieved at the same time.

"You good Lil' Brother?" he asked me as he continued to stare at the heavy rain.

I nodded. "Yeah. I jus' wish my mama was here."

"How you think we gon' go out when we do?"

I took a deep breath and shook my head. "Man, I hope not like him. That shyt was cold blooded."

He laughed. "He deserved that shyt tho'."

I was never close to my father ever so I didn't argue with Bishop about what he said. I was still angry that he took my mother from me.

"How you think you gon' go out?"

"Man, like Scarface." He said as he laughed, but stayed focused on the rain.

"Scarface, huh?" I laughed with him. "I can't go out like that."

"I can't either on some serious shyt. I know I won't die in jail or at the hands of a bitch ass nigga. I can promise you

that."

I nodded. "I dig that, Bruh."

He was going to get what he wanted too; he wouldn't die at the hands of no bitch ass nigga or in jail.

"Where is he? What happened?" I heard him walk through the kitchen as he headed to the bedroom we were in.

"I don't know what happened." I heard Juicy following behind him sounding a bit nervous.

Bishop walked into the middle of the room and paused when he noticed the room was rearranged and DJ wasn't there. I stared at him through the crack of the door as I stood behind it waiting to see if he was going for his gun or not.

He faced the wall and didn't move as he dropped his head.

"You here Little Brother?" he asked still facing the wall.

I stepped to the right slowly coming from behind the door with my gun in my right hand aligned with my right thigh as he put his hands in the air and slowly turned around to face me.

Juicy was standing in the doorway behind me to my left and out of my peripherals I watched her pull her gun from underneath her shirt behind her back. My mother slowly opened the closet door and stepped out of it, but behind me to my right.

Bishop smiled. "Hey Peaches."

"Hello Bishop. Long time no see."

He nodded. "Lookin' good."

"You're lookin' fucked." She smirked.

He laughed and looked back to me directly in my eyes.

"You knew I was comin' for you after that shyt in Miami." I started.

He nodded. "Yeah I knew. I tried to get you before you got me on Hayden, but Dude was too scary to go through wit' it. I guess this was my fate." He said shrugging.

I laughed. "Dude? See that's what happen when you send your bitch to do a man's job. You woulda been better off doin' it yourself."

"You right. Are you goin' to take care of DJ for me?"

I nodded. "Of course."

He nodded his head repeatedly as he looked around DJ's room. "You know that I never did shyt to hurt you intentionally right?"

"I know. And you know I have to follow the

rules since you came to my house right?"

He nodded as he slowly moved to his knees keeping his hands in the air.

"I'm sorry for what my father did to you."

His eyes widened and tears started coming down slowly.

"If I could have killed him myself 'bout you I would have."

Tears started to come down my face slowly too. I was about to kill my brother and I knew this would be a death that haunted me forever.

"Where's Stalyce?" my mother asked.

Bishop kept facing me, but his eyes went to my mother. "She knows you're lookin' for her. She knew when you came home you would be."

"Where the fuck is she Bishop!" my mother yelled.

"I sent her away when I found out you were here. You won't find her. I had to protect her."

My mother was furious when he said that and walked over to him quickly and with her right arm she quickly raised it and down backward in a fast motion hitting him in his lip with the butt of the gun.

Bishop took the hit like a G and turned his head back toward her. "I'm sorry."

"Respect. That's your mother; you did what you were supposed to do. But I will find her and I will kill her."

They stared at each other briefly and she moved back to where she was standing at on my right. Juicy then moved up and wiped his face of the tears. The way she was looking at him I could tell that no matter what her mouth said, she still loved him.

"Nah. No tears." She said softly. "You weren't cryin' when you was doin' all the shyt you was doin'!"

"I'm sorry for everything Ju. You know my love for you is real."

She didn't say a word they just locked eyes. I didn't need her turning this moment into their own love scene so pulled her back and pushed her to the side.

"I love you, Little Brother." He said as he cried some more.

My tears matched his and I tried to hold them back, but I knew I couldn't because of our history.

"I love you too, Bishop."

He closed his eyes and I let two go in his chest. His body jerked and he opened his eyes as we watched the blood began to leak out and he made eye contact with me. I didn't break the stare as I passed my gun to my left across my body to Juicy.

She was crying too as she took the gun and stepped in front of me to face him. I pulled her a few steps back from him so that they weren't too close. He was beginning to wobble his body slightly with his hands to his side. I could tell the metal was beginning to kill him slowly, but he was trying to fight it.

"I love you Bishop." She whispered as she leaned in and kissed his cheek then stepped back and shot him in between his eyes.

He was done then. He took his last breath as his body collapsed to the floor and Juicy turned her face toward me and dropped her head into my chest crying. I held her because even though we all did some fucked up shyt to each other, there was no denying we loved each other deep down inside. We were all we knew at one point.

My mother took the gun with a cloth and began to wipe it clean. "Time to go." She said.

My mother was the only one emotionless after watching Bishop die. She knew him since he was born, but she somehow had sealed her heart to their entire family was she was locked up.

Juicy continued to cry in my arms holding onto me tight. "I can't believe we jus' did that!"

"Let's go." I said releasing her grip on me.

"Where am I supposed to go?" she asked sounding lost.

I knew she couldn't come with me and I hadn't thought that far in advance about where she would go once this was over.

"Wherever you want."

She pulled away and shook her head at me as her watery puffy eyes looked like they held so much pain.

"Take me to my son."

I nodded. "Okay."

"It a be cleaned up." My mother assured me.

"Okay. Call me when you done. Imma take her to DJ."

She nodded as she put on her gloves.

I had Juicy follow me to the hotel in Akron and was trying to figure out how to keep it from being a scene once these two met. I called Aariona immediately.

"Hey." I said softly.

"Hi."

"What the kids doin'?"

"Both are sleep." She continued to be short with me.

"It's over." I said to tell her what she wanted to hear.

"Are you ok?"

"No. But I will be."

"Where are you?"

"Headed there."

"Good."

"I have Juicy following me. She has to get DJ." I said quickly throwing that in there.

"Mmm. Okay." She said hanging up the phone.

I knew that she would have some sort of attitude still and I still couldn't find a way to tell her about the other baby with the responses she was giving me.

I called Juicy phone to make sure she was cool following me still.

"You good?"

"No."

"Me either."

"We really did that?"

"Yep. We had too. He was so far gone he would have got us sooner or later."

"So your father is the one that turned him out, huh?"

"Yeah. Shyt fucked up ain't it?"

"He ever, you know?"

"Nah. Hell nah. I ain't even know 'bout Bishop until recently. He turned that nigga out you was wit' too from what I was told."

"What? Who, Tae?" she sounded surprised.

"Yeah, Tiffany uncle."

"Damn. He said your father took somethin' from him a long time ago, but wouldn't ever say what it was. Now it makes sense why he was after you so hard."

"All this shyt started from Stalyce and Peaches fucked up life. We just cleaned up the mess."

"Damn." She said.

"It's over now." I assured her.

"What 'bout Tiffany?"

"Damn. I don't know. You should be finding her a good ass lawyer tho', Juicy. You fucked that one up and you need to clean it up."

"You right." She didn't argue about it.

"Look, when we go in here I don't want no shyt about my wife, or you saying anything crazy to her ok?"

"Okay."

I parked in the garage of the hotel and she parked next to me. I stood by the elevator waiting for her and when she got out she had her hair fixed and some gloss on and apparently switched shirts. I laughed to myself. She just had to fix herself up when I told her she was meeting my wife.

We walked into the penthouse suite and it was quiet and dark with a few lamps on. DJ was laying on the couch sleep and Solomon was in the bassinet.

"Aariona?" I called out quietly so I wouldn't wake

the kids.

Juicy walked over to Solomon before she even looked at DJ. I shook my head at how thirsty she was to see him. I knew she was lookin' to see if he looked like me.

Aariona came out the bedroom and she was cleaned up too. Her hair was combed and hanging down and she had on her Victoria Secret's *Pink* lounge wear. She had on gloss and her favorite diamond earrings I bought her.

I stared at her because she looked beautiful and her body didn't even look like she had a baby a few days ago. They were both beautiful women, but I was in love with Aariona so her beauty was magnified to me.

Neither one of them looked at me, they both stared at each other. It was like they were trying to see what I saw in the other because they were both completely different women.

Once Aariona was done with her stare she walked over and hugged me and kissed me in front of Juicy. I knew what she was doing and I thought she was childish for it, but she was my wife and she had that right if she wanted to do that.

"You ok, baby?" Aariona asked me in the sweetest voice I've heard from her in a while.

I raised a brow at her. She was going hard right now. "I'm good."

"Hello." She finally said to Juicy.

"Hello." She said back in a snide manner.

"Juicy, huh?" Aariona asked as she walked closer to her.

"Yep. And you are? Black has never mentioned you to me." She said trying to be funny.

Aariona gave me a look and focused back on Juicy. "Well you know when something is so precious you don't share it with everyone. I'm his *wife,* Aariona."

I smiled at the way she handled that. Juicy would have flown off the handle and called her all kind of bitches and probably tried to cut her up. Juicy had no comeback for what Aariona said to her and I was glad because I didn't want to break up a fight tonight.

"Congratulations on the marriage and the new baby."

Aariona smirked. "Thanks."

"That's a lot to have going. To be a new wife, new mother, *new step-mother*."

I knew where she was going when she added the step mother part in and I gave her a look to stop.

"Step-mother? No, we have Solomon and that's enough for our family. I mean DJ is welcome anytime, but I wouldn't try and be his mother. He has you."

Juicy smiled. "I wasn't in reference to my son. I

meant your step-daughter." She said as she crossed her arms feeling like she won.

Aariona's face dropped. "What is she talking about?"

"I should smack the shyt out of you." I said staring Juicy in her eyes.

She quickly removed her smile when she realized that trying to piss off Aariona was about to cost her the front row of teeth she had.

"Devon, what is she talking about?"

I took a deep breath and dropped my head. "I just found out I have a daughter."

She stepped away from me and put her hands on top of her head as she exhaled loudly. "I did not sign up for this!"

"Aariona, please."

"No, Devon! What's next?" she asked coming back face to face with me. "Huh?"

I didn't respond. I was speechless and didn't want to tell her nothing is next and then it end up being a lie.

"And who is the mother of this child?"

"Tiffany."

"Who the hell is she?" she asked throwing her arms in the air.

"You don't know her. She wasn't important."

"She was important enough to have your baby!"

"I didn't even know she had my baby until I came back here!" I defended myself.

"How old is this baby?" she asked crossing her arms.

"A few months."

Her eyes widened. "What! This is a *new* baby?"

"Are you goin' to leave me?" I asked needing to know.

"Where is her mother?"

"Jail."

"Are you kidding me, Devon? Who are you?"

"I'm the man you fell in love with and married."

"No. You're not."

"Are you goin' to leave me?" I asked again.

I was furious Juicy let this out, but relieved that it was finally out the bag.

"I'm going to bed." She said and walked away and slammed the door to the bedroom.

"Why would you do that?" I asked Juicy.

"I thought she knew by now."

"No you didn't because if she knew there would be no reason for you to bring it up to her. It's time for you to go." I said using my thumb to point the way out.

She threw her hands up. "Go where? I have no place to go remember!"

I shook my head because she was right. "Let's go downstairs and get you a room. Stay the fuck away from this suite, we clear?"

She nodded.

I went and got her a room for a few days so she could rest and figure out where she was going from there and went back to my suite to take a shower and check on my mother.

"You done?"

"Yeah. Everything good." She said as she hung up the phone.

I hopped in the shower letting the water run on my face as I closed my eyes thinking about everything that went on since we been here. Cleveland was toxic for me, it was a cancer that if I stayed any longer would eat me alive. When I was in Miami I was at peace. I needed to get back to my new home fast and take my family. My wife and I never argued this much.

I remember when I killed Kisha that she was a face I saw when I closed my eyes at night. None of the others I ever killed ever popped into my mind; ever. But as I stand in this shower with my eyes closed now the only face I see is Bishop's.

Tiffany

I couldn't even focus on what was being said while I was in court. I would hear things randomly like my name or Keyona's name or murder, but never paid attention to what was actually being said.

I sat there in a daze feeling numb. I felt like I was losing my mind and the whole court thing was surreal. They didn't even want me to give me a bond. First time offender and they felt like I was a real threat. They painted a picture of me being some kind of monster. I maybe be many things, but the things they said about me weren't even close to who I was.

I gave up in court because if I were on the jury I would have believed the things they were saying too. I zoned out and started to think about my daughter and how she would feel knowing her mother was going to jail for most of her life.

She probably didn't know I was her mother anyway. I never spent time with her and I started regret the fact I didn't. I remember trying to get pregnant with her; tricking Black into cumming in me because he thought I was on birth control and when I finally got what I wanted I didn't even want her or give her the love she deserved.

The more I sat there and thought about it the more I thought fuck it maybe I deserve to be where I am. Karma never comes back the way you put it out and I was definitely reaping what I sowed.

I know the jury thought I was crazy because no matter what they said I never made a face. I didn't show any emotions or blink an eye. I just wanted it to all end.

God if you get me out of this one I swear I will be a better mother. I will go to school and do my best to change.

I just sat there praying over and over in my mind hoping that He would hear me and save me from this madness I created.

"You get to go home." I heard the lawyer say breaking me out of my thoughts.

"What?" I asked hoping I heard him right.

"I told you I would be able to find a way out of this." He said smiling confidently.

I redirected my attention to the judge and the jury. The whole court session had passed me by and I didn't hear a word of it. I left my fate in this amateur lawyers hands and he came through for me.

I thought hearing that would make me run out of the court room, but I couldn't move. I was in shock that I had my freedom back and wondered if it was because I told God I would change or pure luck.

"But how?" I still didn't understand.

"Weren't you listening?" he frowned at me.

I shook my head.

He shook his at me. "Tiffany, they don't have a murder weapon and the evidence they were trying to use against you deeming you as the murderer had been tampered with. Now it's not over yet, but the murder charges against you are dropped."

I couldn't believe my ears. "Are you serious?"

He nodded.

"What now?"

"I would go enroll in school and find a job if I were you. We need to make you look like you aren't apart of that life at all and you were just in the wrong place at the wrong time."

I nodded because that's what I planned to do. I wasn't sure about the job part though. I was addicted to my lifestyle and working a *job* wasn't part of that lifestyle.

I turned my attention to the spectators in the court and there was Juicy and Black sitting there. I wondered how long they had been there.

I continued to stare at them as I talked to my lawyer. "You know how long they been there?" I asked.

He looked at them and then at me. "That's who has

been paying me the last few days to get you out of this."

"What?" I looked him in his eyes. "Who?"

"Those two right there." He nodded his head in their direction.

"Mmm. She the reason I'm in this shyt to begin with." I snapped.

"She told me. She also told me who really did it." He said letting me know he knew the real truths I kept out.

"So now what?"

"I motion for the courts to go after him and not you."

"How much they pay you?" I was curious.

"20% above my fee."

I widened my eyes. "Who paid that? Him or her?"

"She brought me money one day he came the next."

I was shocked and figured Juicy did that out of guilt. I was still pissed at her for it though.

"They goin to take you back to let you out and we'll be in touch." He said shaking my hand.

I nodded. "Thank you."

He walked away as Juicy and Black stood up and moved toward the door. I was shocked Black was even there at a court house.

He nodded his head at me and I didn't nod back I just stared and wondered what made him help me after I shot at him. Perhaps he knew Teonna was his and did it for her. Whatever the reason was I was going to find out.

Processing to release me didn't go as quick as it did when they brought me in. They made me sit for a few hours before I was finally released. I didn't expect to see the two of them when I came out, but they were still there waiting for me.

I walked over to them and stared Juicy in her face. My first instinct was to punch her in the mouth, but we were still too close to jail and after my experience here I never ever wanted to return.

"I'm really, *really* sorry." She started before I could say anything to her.

I turned and looked at Black and he was standing there with his arms crossed. I couldn't tell what he was thinking.

"Thank you." I said to him.

He nodded. "I did it for your daughter."

"Our daughter." I said correcting him.

He didn't respond.

"Now what?" I asked them.

"Now, I take you home to her so I can go back to Miami." He said.

"What 'bout Teonna?"

"We take the test then go from there."

"You know she yours or you wouldn't be here right

now." I snapped.

He laughed. "We still takin' a test."

I looked at Juicy because I knew she was the reason he didn't trust anyone's word anymore when it came to that.

"Okay." I said giving in.

He had that right to feel like that about me too because of what Juvey and I had going.

"You ready?" he asked. "I have a flight to catch.

"You leavin' today?" Juicy asked sounding like she was about to cry.

He nodded. "She free, you cool; I did what I needed to do. I need to take my wife and son home."

"Your what?" I asked.

"Wife and son." He repeated.

"Son?"

"Yes."

"Wow. How old is he?" I needed to know.

"Few weeks now."

"Wow. I'm ready to go home to my child please." I said ending the conversation.

He didn't say anything he just turned and started to walk away and Juicy and I followed.

After about 30 minutes of complete silence on the

way to my house all I could think about is a hot shower and laying in my bed and sleeping for a day. My mother never came to court not once or to visit me while I was there. When I walked in the house Juicy and Black came in with me. He wanted to see Teonna and since Juicy was with us she came in anyway.

My mother was sitting on the couch crying rocking back and forth and Teonna was in the playpen screaming. It was like she didn't hear her at all. I was confused as I walked over and picked Teonna up to calm her down.

Black directed his attention to my mom. "You ok?"

She looked up at him and cut her eyes. She knew who he was, so it wasn't like this was their first encounter.

"Why didn't you come to court?" I asked her as I bounced Teonna in my arms as she began calm down.

"They found my brother!" she screamed.

"Huh? What are you talkin' 'bout?"

"Your Uncle Tae-" she started to hyperventilate as she was telling me. "Somebody slit his throat."

My eyes widened and I looked at Juicy and Black. Black folded his arms and had the same facial expression he always has. Juicy dropped her head when I looked at her and I knew then she had something to do with it. I wasn't even mad at her either. I was surprised that she had something to do with it because of how much she loves him. From the way her body language changed I could tell it bothered her that he was gone.

I on the other hand didn't feel any remorse for him. It bothered me that my mother was hurt behind it because I know how close they were.

"He didn't bother nobody!" she wailed. "Niggas always wanna take the next hard workin' man's life cause they jealous!" she continued to cry.

I didn't say a word because I knew she didn't know what he *really* did to get his money. She always felt like he was the one who made it out of their family by living right and grindin' for his. She had no idea that he was a professional robber and I wasn't going to be the one to tell her.

"I'm sorry Ma." I said trying to sound sincere as I could be.

She got up and ran up to her room and I heard the door slam. I sat on the couch and laid Teonna across my lap as I bounced her to keep her staying calm.

"Which one of y'all did it?" I asked looking directly at Black.

He laughed. "Nah, playa, not me this time."

I looked at Juicy. "You?"

She nodded. "After you told me he robbed me I knew I had to get him and I needed to make it right with you."

"But how? He is always prepared for that kind of shyt." I said in disbelief.

"I told you that we loved each other. It *was* real between us." She insisted.

I didn't argue with her about it. She needed to believe that they were in love and because she just killed someone she loved I allowed her to continue believing it. I knew better though.

I noticed Black didn't say anything, but stayed staring at Teonna.

"You wanna hold her?" I finally asked.

He paused for a minute then nodded. I handed her to him and she went to him without a fuss and laid her head on his chest.

"Both of your kids look like you." Juicy blurted out.

"I see." He agreed.

"How are you goin' to start a relationship wit' her from Miami?" I asked.

"I'll come get her from time to time."

"What if she lived with you? At least until I finish school." I asked.

He looked at me then at her. "I have to talk to my

wife about it."

I rolled my eyes. I still couldn't believe he was married with a child. I wanted to be a mother to her, but I really didn't know how to and since he had a family I thought she might be better off in another state with a fresh start to a better life than we had.

"I'll talk to her." He said after looking at my facial expression.

"Okay."

He handed Teonna back to me once she fell asleep.

"You ready?" he asked Juicy.

She nodded and walked over to me. I stood up to let them out and she reached in and hugged me. I started to pull back, but instead I hugged her back.

"I'm sorry, Tiff for everything I put you through. It's jus' hard to tell who really down for you and who ain't ya' know?"

I nodded. "Yeah I know. I'm sorry for everything I did too."

"Call me if you ever need me or jus' wanna talk, okay?"

I nodded. "Okay."

Black stood by the front door and I walked over to him and tried to feel him out.

"I know this isn't our goodbye because of her." I said

pointing at Teonna. "But I am sorry for everything I did from day one to you."

He nodded.

"Thank you for getting me out of there too."

"It's all good."

I waited to see if he was going to apologize to me, but he didn't so I spoke up about it.

"Uh, don't you have somethin' to say?"

"I'll call you after I talk to my wife."

"Uh, no apology from you 'bout nothin'?" I asked throwing my hands on my hips.

He leaned on the screen door grabbing the handle pushing it open. "Fo' what? I ain't did shyt!" he said smiling as he walked out the door dodging me trying to hit his arm as he said that.

"Asshole." I said laughing at him.

Juicy looked at me and gave me a half smile and walked out. I wondered if she and I would ever see each other again. I knew we may cross paths one day because we held too many secrets between us and we didn't have anyone else now but each other. I just hoped we crossed paths under different circumstances.

Juicy

I had been staying in the hotel for a few weeks since we murdered Bishop. I really didn't know where Stalyce his body and I hadn't been home since we killed him.

DJ didn't mind staying there because he enjoyed the room service and since Bishop's body hadn't been found or anything yet I wondered if it were safe for me to go home.

Black made me pay for Tiffany's lawyer and he didn't bother to put any money down on her case at all. He was there the whole time, but told me since I was the one that put her there I had to pay for her to get out. I don't know how the evidence against her disappeared or what he had done, but somehow Peaches helped him make shyt happen. As long as I made my wrongs right with her and Black I was ok.

I cried myself to sleep every night because I missed Tae so much. It hurt me that I had to kill him, but I knew that he couldn't walk around freely after what he did to me.

Killing Bishop was hard for me too even though I thought it wouldn't be. Peaches was right, when you are in live with someone as long as I was in love with him it wouldn't be as easy as it seemed when I was hating him. Not only had I taking Black away from DJ; but I murdered his real father too.

I wondered how Peaches was going to find Stalyce because she seemed to be on a real mission and Bishop knew it or he wouldn't have sent her away. I got out of the hotel bed and called Black's phone to see if I could go home or if I really had to leave Cleveland.

"Yeah." He answered on the first ring.

"Hey. Busy?"

"Nah, we just got home. What's up?"

"I'm kind of tired of this hotel stuff now. You think it's safe to go home yet?"

"Yeah you should be cool. Jus' keep your eyes open to everything."

"You think Dude or Juvey gon' suspect anything and come for me?" I worried.

"Nah. They don't exist."

I got quiet. I should have known once Bishop told Black that Dude was going to be the one to kill him on Hayden when they met up he was going to find him. Black was so vengeful that if he even *thought* you were coming for him he was going to get you first and even though Dude chickened out since he thought about it he had to go.

"You can sleep with no worries." He assured me.

"Would you like to see DJ sometimes?" I offered.

"Of course."

"Black?"

"Yeah?"

"Thank you."

"Yep." He said and quickly hung up on me.

I packed DJ and I up and rushed home. I wanted to sleep in my own bed and enjoy my own house again. When I walked in it was spotless. There was some kind of cleaning chemical smell I had never smelled before and it made my stomach turn so I cracked a few windows.

I went directly to DJ room and everything was in place like it was before we killed Bishop. I looked at the spot where I watched him fall over at after I killed him and heard the quick sound of the silencer as the bullet rushed through and landed between his eyes replay in my ears. I closed my eyes and a tear fell with it.

I knew I couldn't live here too much longer. I turned the TV on for DJ and grabbed our clothes to wash.

"Be right back after I throw these clothes in the washer."

"Ok, Mommy."

I walked down the basement steps and felt and

uneasy feeling in my stomach and the smell I was smelling got stronger as I got down there. It was like a bunch of chemicals mixed in with a cement smell.

I turned on the light and looked around but didn't see anything so I switched on the rest of the lights as I walked around the basement attempting to locate the smell as I covered my nose with my right hand.

I got closer to the basement wall and noticed it was coming from there and took my left hand as I moved it across the wall slowly trying to figure out what it was then it dawned on me and I jumped back and gasped. Peaches had hid Bishop's body in my basement!

I touched the wall and leaned my head against it as I smacked it a few times and cried. I knew what she was doing. She was making sure I never left this house and she always knew where I was just in case things got bad between us. She was trapping me and I wondered if Black had something to do with that too.

I was officially bound to this house and them for the rest of my life.

Black

It felt great to be back in Miami. The whole scenery had a different feel and my wife was back to her normal self.

We were out in our backyard with our neighbors; Calvin and his wife as if nothing happened recently. I couldn't lie, I felt good after going back and cleaning up some loose ends in Cleveland the last month. Once you get into that lifestyle it can become addictive and it was so natural for me.

I had been trying to talk Aariona into letting Teonna come stay with us after I told Tiffany I would, but she wasn't having it. She would say let her take care of her child like a real mother should and you can get your child when it's your days to.

Maybe because it was all new to her and maybe she would change her mind one day. I did want to get to know my daughter more so I would face time Tiffany when I was in my car or before I went into the gym so I could see her.

She seemed to love seeing my face on Face Time too so it made me smile. I planned to give Aariona a little more time to get adjusted, but little did she know I was getting my daughter. Tiffany agreed to give me full rights and there was no way I was going to pass that up.

"Man, it seemed like you two weren't coming back!" Calvin said as he grabbed a beer out of the cooler and sat on a patio chair next to me.

"Yeah, well her having the baby while we visited our family kind of set us back." I lied.

She rolled her eyes when she heard me say that and continued talking to Calvin's wife while she cooed at Solomon.

"I can imagine. When Aariona told Sandy on the phone she had the baby we knew you probably wanted to stay there so your family could see him for a while."

I nodded and my cell rang interrupting us from talking. It was my mother.

"Let me take this call." I said getting up and walking into the house.

"Hey, Son."

"What's up Lady. I was jus' thinkin' 'bout you."

I could hear the smile in her voice. "I miss you. How is the baby?"

"Active. He seem to be doin' too much before his time."

She laughed. "Sounds like you."

"I told Juicy she could go home, is that cool?" I asked remembering how I forgot to tell her about it.

"Yep. Everything is everything that way."

"I told her that I wanted to get DJ sometimes. I hope she don't be on no bull shyt when it comes to him."

"Nah, she won't be."

"How you so sure?"

"Cause she got three roommates that will keep her company while he gone visiting you." She said sounding a bit distracted.

I was quiet as I tried to think about what she was talking about then it dawned me she hid Bishop, Dude, and Juvey's body at her house. I shook my head. My mother was ill.

"Damn." I laughed. "She know?"

"Uh, I'm almost sure she does now."

"You wild, Ma."

"So how is Aariona?" she asked.

"Still won't budge about Teonna living here."

"I'll talk to her when I get down there."

"When is that?" I wondered because she was supposed to had been came to Miami.

"In a few days."

"Where are you now?" I wondered.

"In Jersey."

"Jersey? What's in Jersey?"

"Stalyce."

I laughed. She meant what she said when she said she was going to find her. "You are something else. Have you found her yet or just have a lead."

"I'm looking at her right now."

"What? Where is she?"

"Laying here on the floor in front of me."

"What! Ma what the hell goin' on?" I asked realizing my mother has officially lost her mind.

"I'll see you in a few days, Son. Kiss my grandbaby for me. Oh and can we go to Zuma when I get there? I hear the food is amazing!" she asked as if life for her right now were normal.

"Ma, I need you to leave Jersey now."

"Good bye, Son. I love you." She said as she hung up on me.

I stood at my kitchen island looking into my backyard at my wife as she entertained our guest wondering what was going through my mother's mind when she just called me. I realized she was so far gone and there wasn't anything I could do to help her.

As I walked back out to the patio and sat down in my chair I stared at Aariona realizing she was more of a blessing than I knew. She was my way out of that life and I looked up to the sky and thanked God for my angel he sent to save me.

ACKNOWLEDGMENTS

It's so many people that I want to acknowledge because there are so many that genuinely love and support me no matter what project I decide to do. The love I have for them is unmeasurable; but the one I have to name is God.

God has blessed me and brought me so far and the relationship I have with Him I wouldn't trade for ANYTHING in this world. If you know me personally you have definitely seen me go through the ringer and when you see me come out please understand and KNOW that it is not me at all, but it is Him who created me in His image; God. All praises go to Him.